BUILDING THE NORTH RIDING

BUILDING THE NORTH RIDING

A Guide to its Architecture and History

Lynn F Pearson

Smith
Settle

First published in 1994 by
Smith Settle Ltd
Ilkley Road
Otley
West Yorkshire
LS21 3JP

ISBN   Paperback   1 85825 032 3
        Hardback   1 85825 033 1

British Library Cataloguing-in-Publication data:
A catalogue record for this book is available from the British Library.

Half-title page: The church of St Helen and the Holy Cross, Sheriff Hutton.
Title page: Looking out over Wensleydale from the keep of Middleham Castle.

Designed, printed and bound by
SMITH SETTLE
Ilkley Road, Otley, West Yorkshire LS21 3JP

Contents

Acknowledgements

The publishers would like to thank the following for permission to reproduce the illustrations listed below:

Les Brandrick, p42*(r)*; Duncombe Park, p75; Sir James Graham Bt, p93; Morritt Arms Hotel, p121; Joseph Rowntree Foundation, pp86*(t)*, 87; Vaux Group, p19.

The line drawings are by Trevor Mitchell. All other illustrations were supplied by the author.

Preface

I NEVER THOUGHT, when observing the spectacular view over the lights of industrial Teesside from my room in the chilly heights of the top floor of Ormesby Hall some seven years ago, that I should one day be writing a guide to the buildings of the North Riding. But my freezing experience — actually a most enjoyable time — at Ormesby has stood me in good stead, and the hours spent exploring further afield have now acquired a new meaning.

To me, the North Riding is much more than architecture alone; it is certainly a place for recreation — toiling up the hills of Colsterdale in the Burn Valley Half-Marathon, or a happy ending to the Coast to Coast Walk at Robin Hood's Bay — to name just a couple. But to go with this potential for outdoor fun, there are always the buildings which form the backdrop: the startling and sometimes funny follies, the romantic ruins, the seaside resorts and, the most interesting discovery for me, the lesser-known buildings of the vales of York and Mowbray.

I hope this book acts as a guide to the architectural history of the North Riding, and tempts you to explore; not all the buildings described are open to the public, but to omit those to which there is no access, would be to ignore some of the most important buildings in the county. Buildings in the care of English Heritage (Byland Abbey, Easby Abbey, Helmsley Castle, Marmion Tower, Middleham Castle, Mount Grace Priory, Pickering Castle, Rievaulx Abbey, Richmond Castle, Wheeldale Roman Road and Whitby Abbey) and the National Trust (Beningbrough Hall, Braithwaite Hall, Moulton Hall, Nunnington Hall, Ormesby Hall, and Rievaulx Terrace and Temples) are open at the times described in their handbooks.

A growing number of sites, some privately-owned, others cared for by trusts or charities, may also be visited, and then there are the garden schemes, which allow visits to gardens and, often, a glimpse of the outside of the house as well. But please, respect the privacy of the owners.

Just a few of these buildings and structures are so far out of the way that walking boots, a map and even, perhaps, a compass are required to find them; having been caught out in hill storms myself, please make sure you go well-equipped when visiting these peculiarly inspiring places. But whatever you visit, I am sure you will agree that the North Riding has some of the greatest architecture in the country. My own favourites are the collection of follies and monuments to be found on the moors and dales, some totally inaccessible; but Castle

Howard is unbeatable as a summation of the power of architecture in the landscape.

There is always a lot to see in the North Riding, and, as always, many people have helped me in the process of exploration (although any errors which may remain in the text are solely my own): I should like to thank Rose Hill and Steve Jenkinson for much Yorkshire hospitality; Mark Whyman, who answered my obscure queries on the Middlesbrough area with reams of useful material; Philip Brown, for his advice on church tiles; Trevor Ermel of Monochrome for producing brilliant black-and-whites; Jim and Margaret Perry for endless dog-sitting; and, finally, Sue Hudson and the estimable dogs Boots, Socks and Benson, who all enjoy exploring Yorkshire.

For their most welcome advice on the buildings of their areas, I should like to thank the following: the Department of Environment, Development and Transportation (Historic Buildings Section) at Cleveland County Council, Department of Technical Services at Harrogate Borough Council, Chief Economic Development and Planning Officer at Langbaurgh on Tees Borough Council, Economic Development and Planning Department at Middlesbrough District Council, Chief Planning Officer at Richmondshire District Council, Director of Technical Services at Scarborough Borough Council, Chief Planning Officer at Stockton-on-Tees Borough Council, and the District Planning Officer at Teesdale District Council.

I am also grateful to Ruth Annison of W R Outhwaite & Son at Hawes, Hovingham Hall, Andrew Morritt, Messrs D F W and J L Mulley of the Morritt Arms Hotel, North Yorkshire Moors Railway Enterprises plc, R Stewart Ramsdale (Historic Buildings Officer at Cleveland County Council), Ryedale Folk Museum, Sutton Park, and Mr P Townsend of Crakehall Water Mill for their assistance in the preparation of this book. I should also like to thank Trevor Mitchell for producing such excellent drawings.

I am grateful to the following for their courtesy in granting permission to reproduce illustrations: Les Brandrick, Duncombe Park, Sir James Graham Bt, the Morritt Arms Hotel, the Joseph Rowntree Foundation and the Vaux Group.

Lynn F Pearson
Gosforth, Newcastle upon Tyne
1994

THE LAND OF THE IRONMASTERS

Cleveland

HIGHCLIFF NAB comes as a shock to the walker emerging from the surrounding forest; at 750 feet above Guisborough, it offers a captivating view of the market town below, a rocky crag to rest upon and a choice of routes down: through Hutton, where Alfred Waterhouse built one of his earliest country houses, or direct to Guisborough and its priory, or perhaps east along the ridge to the old ironstone-mining villages (and a castle) nearer the coast. The Nab is just one of the many exhilarating viewpoints along the scarp top of the Cleveland Hills, most of which are connected by the Cleveland Way long-distance path.

But to the view. Looking north at Guisborough, on the north-east edge of the market town the remains of Gisborough Priory (an old spelling) may be made out, though at this distance the soaring east end is deprived of its spectacular silhouette. The Augustinian priory was founded around 1119 by a wealthy local baron, Robert de Brus, ancestor of the Scottish King Robert I or Robert Bruce. Partly as a result of the original generous endowment the priory became rich, but was still noted for its strict observance in religious matters. The canons decided to rebuild their first church in the early thirteenth century, and the project was near completion when disaster struck. On the 16th May 1289 the church was burned to its foundations in a fire begun when a workman, who had been soldering lead on the roof of the south transept, neglected to douse his burning coals.

Immediately the canons rebuilt and produced a wonderful work in the Decorated style. The glorious east end can still be seen, its arch framing the countryside to the east. It stands ninety-seven feet high, its full original height, and the central east window, now lacking its lower border, would have measured fifty-six feet top to bottom. This cavernous arch, reaching above the town, is the abiding memory of Guisborough, town and priory; beautiful and a little unfulfilling, but enough to suggest the quality of the original building. It was not enough for the Victorians (or

The great east wall of Gisborough Priory, built after the fire of 1289 which destroyed most of the original church. The cost of rebuilding was an important factor in the decline of the priory's finances during the fourteenth century.

perhaps Georgians), however; at some point in the nineteenth century the wall beneath the window was removed, increasing the undoubted picturesqueness of its aspect. It would never happen in these more regulated times, but the result is a triumph.

Dissolution came to the priory in 1540, and the site, complete with its still-surviving dovecot, was bought ten years later by Sir Thomas Chaloner. The Chaloners took over the canons' role as lords of the manor and built the old hall, which stood south-west of the priory, around the end of the sixteenth century.

At this time Guisborough was an unremarkable but growing market town; its weekly market was granted in 1263 by Henry III. The church of St Nicholas, just north of the priory, dates from about 1500, and is notable for its ten knights carved in stone and stationed on the Brus Cenotaph. The cenotaph commemorates English and Scottish branches of the Brus family and originally graced the priory; it was created around 1520-30 and shows a fine standard of carving.

Guisborough's one main street, Westgate, is a pleasant enough composition, but there is little to detain the traveller (except the thought of John Wesley being almost suffocated by the smell of stinking fish on his second visit to Guisborough in 1761, when he preached in the market place). Beyond the town to east and west, however, lie a pair of interesting country houses.

Gisborough Hall, sited half a mile east of the priory, was built for Admiral Chaloner in 1857 by William Milford Teulon, younger brother of the more famous architect Samuel Sanders Teulon, a thoroughly eclectic stylist. W M Teulon indulged in a little whimsy at Gisborough, designing an oriel window in the form of ship's stern complete with porthole, perhaps at the behest of the admiral. The house was much altered in 1902.

South-west of Guisborough, now almost beside the town's expanding commuter belt estates, stands Hutton Hall, home of Teesside ironmaster and industrialist Joseph Whitwell Pease between 1867 and 1902. (The hall lies beside Hutton Village Road where it heads south into the hills; from the centre of Guisborough, take Hutton Lane south from the west end of Westgate and follow the road left at Hutton Gate.) Joseph Whitwell Pease inherited his wealth from the family firm begun by his great-great-grandfather Edward Pease in Darlington during the mid-eighteenth century. Edward Pease made his mark on the increasingly industrialised textile trade and in 1785 left his only son Joseph a thriving woollen business, which Joseph expanded and diversified to include banking interests.

Joseph's son Edward inherited in 1808, and initially continued to manage the firm with few changes. By 1817 his enthusiasm for business life was declining, and much of his energy was spent on Quaker affairs; his grandfather had joined the Society of Friends before 1735. It was a surprise, then, that Edward (and his second son Joseph) should suddenly become involved in the promotion of the Stockton and Darlington Railway, which eventually opened in 1825. The Pease family invested heavily in the venture, which was the making of their fortune, as the coal-carrying line proved a great success.

Edward Pease died in 1858, although he had vowed never to attend a railway meeting again in 1827, and thence devoted his time to the Society of Friends. Young Joseph took on the business, and proved a successful colliery entrepreneur, banker and railway promoter, as well as becoming one of the founding fathers of Middlesbrough. By the 1850s, Pease industrial and commercial concerns were of substantial financial importance in the North-East. In 1852 the firm of J W Pease & Co was founded to exploit the ironstone deposits of the Cleveland Hills; the firm was managed by Joseph's eldest son, Joseph Whitwell Pease.

J W Pease first developed ironstone workings at Hutton Lowcross, then a tiny village nestling in a valley about a mile to the south-west of Guisborough. By the mid-1870s the firm was the largest ironstone producer in Cleveland.

It is said that Joseph Whitwell Pease chose the site for his family home at Hutton while on a trip to visit his nearby ironstone works. Pease commissioned Quaker architect Alfred Waterhouse to design the mansion, and planning began in 1864. Lancashire-born Waterhouse had cousins within the Pease family, and this sizeable commission undoubtedly assisted his early career, although he had almost established himself by 1864. He went on to design some of the great monuments of corporate Victorian England, including Manchester Town Hall, a series of Prudential Assurance offices and the Natural History Museum.

Hutton Hall, a rambling red-brick Gothic pile, was completed in 1866 and the family, with their seven children, moved in the following year. The estate covered 2,912 acres and the house, with its 6 reception rooms, 38 bedrooms and dressing rooms, and stabling for 24 horses, cost £88,000.

Unlike their restrained Quaker elders, the Whitwell Peases lived in some style. There were around forty indoor and outdoor servants, and the food was nothing but the best; the weekly menu was constant and the necessary ingredients were obtained irrespective of season. J W Pease also commissioned Waterhouse to design a private railway station, sited to the north of the hall, and a reading room for Hutton village. At Hutton, Pease enjoyed country life to the full. Apart from the traditional pursuits of hunting and shooting, there were the pleasure grounds with ornamental walks, an Italian garden, acres of parkland and numerous glasshouses.

But the story did not have a happy ending. Perhaps J W Pease was not quite the businessman his father had been, perhaps events — such as the 'iron smash' of the late 1870s, in which overseas financial crises combined with competition from steel to reduce railway revenues dramatically — turned against the Pease empire, or perhaps the lure of country life distracted J W Pease from the harsh industrial world. By the 1890s Sir Joseph, created a baronet in 1882, was in severe financial difficulties, compounded by a court case involving his niece Beatrice, who had been raised by the Whitwell Peases as their daughter after the death of her father. Beatrice was convinced that Sir Joseph was holding back money due to her from her father's will; in 1898 judgement went in her favour, badly damaging the reputation of Sir Joseph. Worse was to come, when in 1902 the Pease family bank was found to be insolvent. Sir Joseph was forced to sell Hutton Hall, and moved to his summer home at Falmouth, where he led a 'dismal' life and died of heart failure on the 23rd June 1903.

About a mile east of Guisborough, down a lane leading north off the A173, is Tocketts Mill, a working watermill dating from around 1810, with a contemporary mill house; the mill was restored in the 1970s. The pitchback waterwheel takes water from Tocketts Beck via a small aqueduct passing through the mill.

A couple of miles further along the A173 lies Skelton; on its western edge, just north of the main road, stands All Saints Old Church,

All Saints Old Church,
Skelton, built in 1785,
probably at the expense of
John Hall Stephenson of
nearby Skelton Castle. The
simple design may have
originated with a contemp-
orary pattern book.

A gravestone at All Saints Old Church, Skelton; there are pirates' graves in this secluded churchyard, which lies west of the village.

now cared for by the Redundant Churches Fund. All Saints was built to a medieval plan and the present building includes some medieval stonework, but it largely dates from 1785. This was probably the second rebuilding of the original church. There is a venetian window and a castellated tower, while the dark pink interior holds a fine array of joinery, including a three-decker pulpit, box pews and a tiered gallery. The seating arrangements enabled the whole of the congregation to face the pulpit rather than the altar, which seems almost excess to requirements. Skelton expanded after 1872 as a consequence of the opening of several ironstone mines near the village, and the old church was replaced by the more central and larger new All Saints in 1881-4.

A little to the north of the old church is Skelton Castle, built around 1794 on a natural promontory, the site of a twelfth century castle; its castellated south front is the work of Durham architect Ignatius Bonomi and dates from 1809-14. The moat, created in the eighteenth century, encloses over five acres of land in the shape of a lozenge, with the castle sited at its northern tip. Its owner in the latter part of the eighteenth century was John Hall Stephenson, who spent part of his inherited fortune on hiring Sir John Soane to build the stables at Skelton in 1787. Hall Stephenson happily squandered the remainder of his wealth on drinking and other entertainments; this was part of his pursuit of enjoyment, which he declared to be his sole aim in life.

Hall Stephenson built Sterne's Well, a small, Classical temple, about half a mile to the south (off Back Lane, on the south-western edge of Skelton), which sheltered the source of the castle's water supply. Hall Stephenson and the innovative writer Laurence Sterne were close friends, once indulging in a chariot race along Saltburn sands, and the verse which decorates the well head, from whence the 'prattling waters' spring, is doubtless by Sterne's hand.

Head back along the A173 west of Guisborough to pass below Cleveland's greatest natural landmark, the remarkable cone of Roseberry Topping. It stands half a mile south-east of Newton under Roseberry (from whence it may be scaled), but its craggy silhouette is visible for miles around. At only 1,050 feet above sea level the peak reaches no great height, but its position as an outlier of the Cleveland Hills has ensured the wonderfully panoramic views from its summit. A sandstone cap has preserved its curious shape, which is partly the result of ironstone excavations.

At Great Ayton we encounter the River Leven, flowing peaceably beside High Street from its source in the hills to the east. The Leven flows to meet the Tees just downstream from Yarm, first passing through the centre of Stokesley, about three miles south-west of Great Ayton.

The market and now commuter town of Stokesley presents a pleasant aspect, with a happy mix of Georgian and Victorian houses and commercial buildings, and assorted footbridges crossing the still-small river. Three miles north of Stokesley, just west of the A172, where it meets the edge of Middlesbrough at Nunthorpe, stands Grey Towers House, marooned in the grounds of old Poole Hospital. This impressive, towered, Gothic mansion, built in 1865-7 by John Ross of Darlington, was the home of ironmaster Sir Arthur Dorman between 1895 and 1931.

West of Stokesley the Leven becomes enmeshed in a series of wooded meanders, overlooked near Middleton-on-Leven by Castle Hill, where the Normans built Castle Levington. It can be reached from Stokesley by way of Hutton Rudby to the west; from there, follow the by-road heading north for Middleton and bear left on the Yarm road. Immediately across the Leven at Foxton Bridge, a bridlepath will take the walker the mile or so north to Castle Hill. This impressive mass rises 125 feet above the river and measures nearly 180 feet across. It is still topped by the remains of an earthwork known as a ringwork, a combination of bank and ditch, which once enclosed a timber castle. Both the ringwork and motte, or mound, were common Norman defensive structures.

Yarm, where Yarm Bridge over the Tees marks the North Riding border with County Durham, lies only three miles north-west of Foxton Bridge. Entering Yarm via the A67 brings the traveller out at the southern end of gently curving High Street, almost half a mile of mainly Georgian terraced houses and inns which have resisted much modern development.

Indeed, Yarm was the premier port of the Tees, exporting corn and lead, during the Georgian period, although the town's most prosperous years were during the fourteenth century, and then around 1660-1720. Bishop Walter Skirlaw built the medieval market town's bridge about 1400 — though it has been much changed since — and until Stockton Bridge was built in 1771 it was the lowest crossing point on the river. The Durham to York road used the Yarm route, which explains the presence of the numerous coaching inns which line High Street; the little town had sixteen inns in 1848, when its population was only around 1,600.

The brick-built town hall, sited on an island in the middle of High Street — as was the habit in the North Riding — was erected in 1710 as a tolbooth, where market administration took place. Originally its ground floor arcade was open, housing sellers of dairy produce and giving access to the stairs leading to the floor above.

Foremost amongst the High Street inns is the Ketton Ox, a four-storey pilastered structure dating from about 1670. Blank, oval windows in its attic storey give the façade a striking appearance. The inn was named after a famous shorthorn reared near Darlington in 1796. At its death the beast weighed 220 stone and its owner refused to sell it for £2,000,

A massive advertisement for the railway engineers Thomas Grainger and John Bourne is displayed on the side of their Yarm Viaduct, built in 1849-52 for the Leeds Northern Railway to carry the track across the Tees. The central spans of the viaduct, visible from Yarm Bridge, come complete with an inscription which reads: 'Engineers: Thomas Grainger & John Bourne. Superintend: Joseph Dixon. Contractors: Trowsdale, Jackson & Garbutt 1849.'

about 100 times the average value of an ox at that time.

The inn was notorious for illegal cock-fighting in the late nineteenth century. The fights took place in a cockpit on the top floor, built after the sport was prohibited in 1849. In an adjacent room was the disused old cockpit, which could be shown to the raiding constabulary whilst fight spectators escaped via a trap-door to the floor below. The birds themselves were dropped down a chute into the yard.

At the northern extreme of the nostalgic vista of High Street a shock awaits; just west of Yarm bridge is the enormous Yarm Viaduct, invisible from the centre of the Georgian town. Its forty-three arches trudge almost directly north-south from Egglescliffe, on the north bank of the river, nearly half a mile to a point near the southern end of High Street.

The viaduct was built in 1849-52 by the Leeds Northern Railway to connect Thirsk and Northallerton with Stockton and the north. It was constructed of red brick apart from the two stone arches which span the river; in their central spandrel is a suitably huge inscription naming the viaduct's engineers and contractors. Thomas Grainger, its leading engineer, was killed in an accident on the Leeds Northern Railway shortly after the completion of the viaduct.

The great brick arches come between Yarm's High Street and its church, which stands beside the Tees on West Street (take Low Church Wynd or any of the streets leading west from High Street). St Mary Magdalene, with its peculiar Norman west front, is a 1730 rebuilding of a twelfth century stone church. There is more fortress than church about the appearance of the west front, and a thirteenth century elongated oval window standing vertically under the tower adds to the odd effect. This window originally opened on to the nave. The interior is mostly a reconstruction job dating from 1878, though a south window of 1768 by William Peckitt of York survives, showing a weighty Moses on Mount Sinai.

The Wesleyan chapel, by the riverbank to the east of High Street opposite the town hall, was erected in 1763 and is the oldest octagonal Methodist church in the country which has remained in continuous use. Wesley himself visited Yarm on nineteen occasions between 1748 and 1788, but the chapel pulpit from which he preached was removed during enlargements in 1815; the Gothic extension was added in 1873.

The chapel can best be seen from the riverside walk, which continues via Yarm Bridge to the parish church on the far side of High Street. Yarm's geographical position, nestling within a loop of the Tees, has led to several instances of flooding, most notably in November 1771 when Pennine storms caused an inundation of twenty feet of water in some parts of the town. The church pews were found floating in nine feet of water. Seven people drowned, though many were rescued by folk from Stockton, and the total loss was put at £7,000. Yarm was last flooded in March 1881.

From Yarm it is only seven miles across country to the centre of Middlesbrough, but few footpaths cross the intervening expanse of farmland, industrial estate and suburbs. Roads, however, have proliferated, offering a choice of routes to the North Riding's largest town, but the most scenic and historic introduction is to take the railway, although this does involve a brief excursion into County Durham.

Yarm's own railway station was sited on the north bank of the river, just over Yarm Bridge, due to the presence of the viaduct. Since the closure of this station, prospective passengers must trek another mile to Allens West by crossing the bridge, following the A67 Nook Road, then bearing right into Durham Lane. From this bleak and windswept halt, a fairly frequent service trundles along beside the Tees towards Middlesbrough.

The journey lasts a quarter of an hour, and provides a potted history of the making of Middlesbrough, from river improvements and railways, to Tees bridges and the old town centre.

The railway line returns to Yorkshire at Thornaby-on-Tees, vaulting the river on the site of the very first suspension railway bridge; this opened in 1830 but was replaced in 1842 as it had become unsafe. The Victorian Renaissance hulk of Thornaby's Town Hall stands almost beside the station on Railway Terrace. It was built in 1891-2 by West Hartlepool architect James Garry.

After Thornaby the unwitting passenger is travelling across flat land which almost constitutes an island; to the north is the Tees, but this section is actually a canal, the Portrack Cut, excavated in 1829-31. This cut, and its predecessor the Mandale Cut (1810), together reduced the distance between Stockton and the sea by three miles. The redundant meanders still exist in part to the south of the railway line. The river improvements were the work of the Tees Navigation Company,

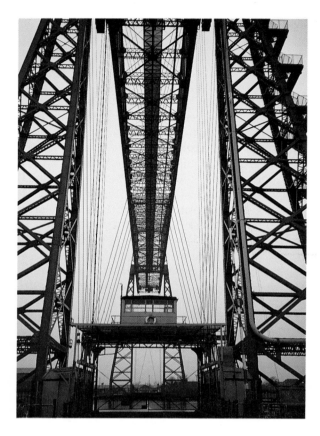

The Transporter Bridge across the Tees at Middlesbrough was opened in 1911. Its memorable silhouette has now become a symbol of the borough.

The huge, blue towers of Newport Bridge, Middlesbrough, rise above the Tees. It opened in 1934, replacing a ferry service, and is still in use as a road bridge, although its deck lifting mechanism no longer functions.

formed in 1805 largely by Stockton interests to further the prospects of their port.

Onward to Middlesbrough, and the railway ducks under the soaring A19 viaduct as one of the town's two immense bridges comes into view; this bulky blue giant is Newport Bridge, a road bridge opened in 1934 which solved

the problem of allowing shipping passage by simply lifting its entire deck ninety-nine feet into the sky. Local steel manufacturers Dorman Long & Co were the constructors, and it was the first vertical lift bridge to be built in England. The 260 foot long deck could be fully raised in around a minute and a half;

this last occurred on the 18th November 1990, after which the deck was fixed in the 'down' position. The obtrusive (and now redundant) lifting mechanisms on the bridge towers render the structure ugly but memorable.

North of Newport Bridge the railway veers away from the river towards the town, but the outline of Middlesbrough's other and better-known bridge may be seen briefly above the buildings.

This is the Transporter Bridge, a fantastic cantilever construction designed by Cleveland Bridge and Engineering Limited and opened in 1911, when it replaced a ferry service across the Tees. Here the deck is tiny, a mere platform which can carry up to nine cars or 600 foot passengers, and swings out across the river suspended by cables from the transporter carriage on the bridge itself. The bridge is 160 feet above the high-water level, and an electric motor on the south bank powers the transporter, which can heave the deck across the Tees in about two and a half minutes. The elegant, latticed-steel bridge in the sky is a tremendous sight from afar, and, at eighteen pence a head for pedestrians, the trip over the water must be one of the best bargains in the North Riding.

And so the train enters Middlesbrough Station, sited just south of the original town centre. The history of modern Middlesbrough really begins in 1827, when the directors of the Stockton and Darlington Railway decided upon what was then a tiny hamlet as the site for their new coal-shipping port. This hamlet was not mentioned in the *Domesday* survey, and only from 1119 can it be certain that the site was occupied. Robert de Brus, owner of vast estates in the North of England, then gave a carucate of land (the amount a team of oxen could plough in a season) at Middlesbrough to the monks of Whitby Abbey, on condition that they maintained a presence there.

Life at the tiny, unimportant monastic and farming community of Middlesbrough continued in its quiet way during medieval times, when a substantial church was built. At the Dissolution the lands passed to the Crown and were sold in 1564; the church represented useful building material and had been almost demolished by around 1660. Early seventeenth century Middlesbrough comprised about twenty buildings, but by the mid-eighteenth century the settlement had dwindled to a handful of cottages, and in 1801 the population of Middlesbrough was put at only twenty-five; these were mostly the inhabitants of outlying farms.

By 1827 the hamlet was home to little more than forty people; Joseph Pease inspected it from the Tees on the 2nd August 1828, when he saw bare fields and salt flats which he imagined would soon be overwhelmed by the activities of the 'busy multitude' in the new port. The Stockton and Darlington Railway intended to extend their line from the congested port of Stockton across the Tees to Middlesbrough, providing an improved outlet for coal. The development of Middlesbrough was undertaken by a group of Quaker financiers including Joseph Pease. Their company, formed in late 1828 and known as the Owners of the Middlesbrough Estate, purchased 527 acres of land at the chosen site in 1830. The railway by then reached as far as the coal staithes of Port Darlington, a point just west of Middlesbrough.

The staithes, designed by the railway company's engineer Timothy Hackworth, were huge structures connecting ships and shore. Loaded wagons were raised twenty feet by steam engine to a high-level deck, then pulled along by horse power until above the ship's hatch. They were then swung out on a gantry above the ship and emptied.

Richard Otley, a Darlington surveyor who was secretary to the railway, drew up a plan for Middlesbrough in 1830. It covered twenty-six acres on the site of the original monastic settlement and comprised 125 building plots arranged on a simple grid plan which centred on a square. It also included the burial ground on the site of the medieval church.

The first house was built in West Street in April 1830 by George Chapman, a joiner, whose son was the first child to be born in the new Middlesbrough in August that same year.

The boy was the first of many, as the development of the town proved immediately popular. The Quaker initiative created a whole new working community based on the sea transport of coal. Middlesbrough's population grew to 150 by 1831 and reached a stunning 5,463 by 1841. By 1845, buildings had been erected on almost all the first 125 plots, and further streets had been laid out to the south and east.

Growth continued swiftly as the coal trade prospered and other industries sprang up; the Middlesbrough Pottery was set up in 1834 by Richard Otley, shipbuilding arrived in 1835 and — most importantly — the ironworks of Henry Bolckow and John Vaughan opened in 1841. However, the boom subsided during the 1840s as both pottery and ironworks suffered financial problems, and the town became overcrowded. Growth resumed after the discovery of ironstone deposits in the Cleveland Hills by John Vaughan in June 1850 and a general revival of North-East trade. Ironworks proliferated on Teesside in the 1850s, as technological advances combined with local availability of raw materials; there were twenty-nine blast furnaces on Teesside in 1854, all newly built since 1850.

The population of Middlesbrough had topped 19,000 in 1862 when W E Gladstone described the town as an 'infant Hercules', and reached 39,563 in 1871. By this time the loop of the Tees to the north-west of the town, still marshy fields in 1860, had been filled by ironworks and associated industries. This triangle of land became known as the Ironmasters' District. By 1871 Teesside was responsible for almost a fifth of Britain's iron production.

Expansion in the 1870s slowed down once again, due to depression in the iron trade and the coming of steel, with areas west and south of the town only being developed in the early twentieth century. After the First World War, council estates and private housing began to hem in the interminable rows of terraced housing which constituted so much of the central area of Middlesbrough. The coming of the chemical and petrochemical industries to Teesside did not stop Middlesbrough from going into a decline in the last quarter of the twentieth century, and the disappearance of industrial buildings left gaping holes in the fabric of the townscape which are only just beginning to be redeemed.

The obvious starting point for an exploration of Middlesbrough is the railway station, standing between old and new town centres. Middlesbrough's first railway station was on the 1830 branch line from Stockton and was a simple wooden structure sited close to the Tees on Commercial Street. When a new line was constructed to serve Middlesbrough Dock (another Joseph Pease initiative) in 1842, a temporary halt was created just to the west of the present station site, south of the original town centre and square. The line was extended to Redcar in 1846, and a new station built the following year on the present site. To cope with the ever-increasing numbers of passengers, an excursion station opened in 1874, and then the impressive Gothic vault of the general station in 1877. By this time the line was under North Eastern Railway management, the Stockton and Darlington having amalgamated with the NER in 1863, largely to ward off predator companies.

The station front was designed by William Peachey, the third of the North Eastern Railway company architects. He followed Thomas Prosser, who designed York and Leeds New (1869) stations during his 1857-74 term of office, and Benjamin Burleigh, NER architect in 1874-6, who completed the works at York. Peachey had a similarly short time in the job but produced a surprising number of stations, the best of which was Middlesbrough.

The Gothic station sits on a terrace above an arcade of shops; inside, the booking hall is a contrast to the slightly gloomy exterior, with its airy hammerbeam roof. Originally, waiting passengers were sheltered by the sixty foot high vault of the glazed trainshed roof, designed by W J Cudworth, but after bomb damage during the Second World War this part of the station was demolished.

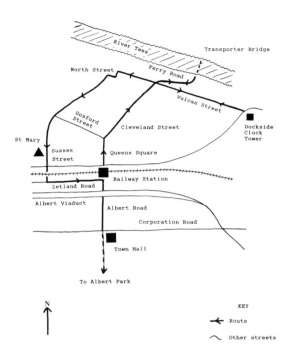

CENTRAL
MIDDLESBROUGH

Leave the station on its north side, heading through the old town centre along Queens Square and Cleveland Street, towards the river front and the Transporter Bridge. This area, known as St Hilda's, was the commercial centre of Middlesbrough when the town was at the height of its powers; nineteenth century confidence and prosperity are typified by the heavily Classical National Provincial Bank of England, on the corner of Cleveland and Gosford Streets. It occupies plots eighty-five

The Dockside Clock Tower on Dock Street. Sadly, the tower is now suffering from neglect.

was once described as the only gentleman living in the town.

The National Provincial bought his house in 1864 and London architect John Gibson, the company's architect from 1864, designed their new bank in 1873. Gibson built a series of banks for the National Provincial, generally producing single-storey, restrained Classical façades even into the 1880s when more picturesque styles were becoming popular. The bank stayed in the Cleveland Street premises until 1936.

From the bank, follow the line of Cleveland Street north-east to the river for an overwhelming view of the Transporter Bridge, but look out for Vulcan Street on the right. At its end is the tall, red-brick Dockside Clock Tower, dating from the late Victorian period, which also acted as a water tower; this reservoir maintained the hydraulic pressure necessary to run the dockside cranes.

On the north side of Vulcan Street stands an intriguing wall, pierced by large oval holes. This is now the sole remains of the Cleveland Salt Works. The works, operational during 1887 to 1947, produced salt by evaporation of brine pumped from the salt beds which underlie the Tees. The Middlesbrough Pottery and the ironworks of Bolckow and Vaughan were also located on Vulcan Street, making it the industrial heart of old Middlesbrough.

Heading back to the west, cross Ferry Road and continue to North Street, where the old custom house, a handsome Greek Revival pile of 1836-7, still stands. It was built as a combination of coal exchange and hotel by Darlington architect George Burlison. Wend your way through the recently-built housing to the south and look out for a tower. It

and eighty-six of the original plan, and replaced a house owned by shipbuilder John Gilbert Holmes. Holmes introduced the shipbuilding industry to Middlesbrough, and, due to his support for the cause of temperance, identifies Middlesbrough's old town hall, located in Market Square, the original centre of the old town. This unassuming Classical building was erected in 1846, although the tower was added later, between 1863 and 1871.

Further south, in Sussex Street, is the red-brick Roman Catholic church of St Mary, with its hammerbeam roof and lengthy, elegant arcades. It was built in 1876-78 by London architects Goldie and Child, a firm which specialised in buildings for the Catholic community. George Goldie (1828-87), grandson of artist and architect Joseph Bonomi, began the practice and later brought in C E Child as chief assistant. After George Goldie's death, Child and George's son Edward Goldie were briefly in partnership before Edward took on the entire practice. Although St Mary was built as a church, it was granted cathedral status in 1879, although this has recently been lost to a modern cathedral at Coulby Newham, on the southern edge of Middlesbrough.

The Transporter Bridge glimpsed through the elegant wall of the Cleveland Salt Works, Vulcan Street, Middlesbrough. Nothing remains of this important works but the wall, with its unusual structure.

From St Mary, an underpass takes the walker south below the railway line; left, on Zetland Road, is the Zetland Hotel, built in 1860. It has an excellent rear bar decorated in late Victorian style, all tiles and mirrors. Next door is Middlesbrough's finest piece of architecture, unfortunately rather over-shadowed by the bulk of the station opposite. The unmistakable scalloped roofline identifies the Bell Brothers' offices, designed in 1881-3 by Philip Webb and built in 1889-91. This is a unique work in that it is Webb's only commercial building.

The firm of Bell Brothers originated on Tyneside in 1842, later expanding into County Durham at Washington and setting up an ironworks at Port Clarence, on the north bank of the Tees opposite Middlesbrough's old town centre, in 1854. In 1867, Isaac Lowthian Bell, son of the company's founder and a brilliant metallurgist, asked the architect Philip Webb to design a clock tower for the Clarence works. Webb, a lover of the countryside whose architecture reflected the English vernacular and was crucial to the development of the Arts and Crafts style, disliked modern industry but had become a friend of the Bell family, probably through mutual acquaintances in London artistic circles. Webb made alterations to Bell's Washington house in 1864-7, and eventually designed several buildings for the Clarence works, all of which were demolished in the 1970s.

Although their works were on the north bank of the Tees, the Bell Brothers' offices had always been in Middlesbrough. By 1881 they needed new premises and Webb was asked for a design, which was complete by 1883; a depression in the iron trade necessitated a break until 1889 before building began.

The distinctive office building was finished in 1891, its façade packed with arches and large windows. Webb concentrated on providing good natural light for all office spaces, and included the latest in technology, by way of lifts, lighting and bells. The building passed to steelmakers Dorman Long in 1902 when Bell Brothers, who had been slow in making the move from iron to steel production, merged with the larger firm.

Zetland Road now opens out into Exchange Place, where, prior to 1985, one would have been confronted by the huge bulk of the Royal Exchange. The exchange was built in 1866-8 to provide a base for traders in pig iron and related commercial activities; it replaced a small exchange in the old town, which had functioned since 1837, and typified the movement south of the town centre. Its architect was Charles Adams of Stockton, who won the commission in a competition which caused intense argument amongst the promoters of the exchange. Adams' design was costly, even though it was built without the tower originally planned, and it failed to generate the predicted income. However, its Italianate bulk symbolised the growth of the new town.

From Exchange Place, head south under the obtrusive road viaduct into Albert Road, which meets Corporation Road at the town hall. Middlesbrough rapidly outgrew its first town hall, and its eventual replacement was again the result of a competition; although Alfred Waterhouse produced plans for a new town hall in 1875 — probably at the behest of Joseph Whitwell Pease — these were never carried out, and Waterhouse acted as assessor for the 1882 contest won by one of his pupils, Darlington architect G G Hoskins.

Building took place between 1883 and 1888; the total cost was £130,000 and the centrepiece of the Gothic design was the great hall, originally decorated with portraits of local worthies. The inevitable tower is 170 feet high.

The grand opening, attended by the Prince and Princess of Wales, was set for the 23rd January 1889, and a jolly time was had by all, with fanfares, processions, quantities of decorations, fireworks, music and general junketing. The royal visit cost the town £2,328, probably good value in terms of publicity as the new town began to emulate the municipal provisions of its older Yorkshire neighbours.

Immediately to the east of the town hall stands the Empire Theatre, its pinky-brown Baroque terracotta façade bringing light relief to uninspiring Corporation Road. It was built in 1897-9 as the Empire Palace of Varieties and was designed by London architect Ernest Runtz. The promoters described the eccentric style of the façade as Spanish Renaissance. Although Runtz was something of a specialist in theatres and later cinemas, his theatre interiors were often disappointing, and the Empire is no exception despite the pleasant balcony plasterwork. However, the towered façade, in terracotta supplied by Doulton of Lambeth, is quite splendid.

South of Corporation Road, row upon row of terraced housing in two intersecting grid plans once extended to Albert Park, a gift to the town from Henry Bolckow in 1867-8. Although the park remains, demolition of most of the terraces began in the mid-1970s. At the time of Bolckow's act of generosity,

'Painting', one of four allegorical figures on the façade of Middlesbrough Town Hall, built in 1883-8. The sculptor was H T Margetson, and the remaining figures symbolised music, literature and commerce.

Waiting at the gates of Albert Park, Middlesbrough, in the early years of the twentieth century. The park was presented to the town by ironmaster Henry Bolckow in 1868.

A winged terracotta beast decorates the façade of the Empire Theatre, Middlesbrough (left), which faces the town hall. The Empire, built in 1897-9, was an early work by the London architect and theatre specialist Ernest Runtz.

open countryside with scattered villages lay beyond the park; Acklam, just over a mile to the south, was centred on Acklam Hall (now part of Kings Manor School on Hall Drive). The hall was built around 1680 for Sir William Hustler, and has splendid joinery and rich plasterwork, including suspended doves and griffins; it was extended in 1845, and again in 1910-12, when additions were made under the direction of York architect Walter Brierley. The standard of the twentieth century decorative work almost matches that of the original.

From the mid-nineteenth century, Middlesbrough's outlying villages rapidly became populated with industrialists who could afford to move away from the source of their wealth. Bolckow moved out to Marton (three miles from the town centre on the A172), building Marton Hall in 1854-7 and enlarging it in 1867-75; Royal Exchange architect Charles

Adams may have designed the later work. The interior was finely decorated with much marble and assorted foreign objets.

Nearby was Gunnergate Hall, a Gothic pile built for Bolckow's partner John Vaughan by

The Zetland Hotel in the industrial suburb of South Bank, Middlesbrough, around the turn of the century; the terraced houses and pub have now been demolished.

Darlington architect James Pigott Pritchett II in 1858. Immediately after Vaughan's death in 1868, his son Thomas embarked upon enlargements; building continued until about 1874 and included a £50,000 billiard room hung with vast paintings. Thomas Vaughan's enjoyment of his estate was brief, as the family firm went under and the house was sold off around 1879.

Both Marton and Gunnergate Halls, built with new money, have now been demolished, but just to the east of their sites still stands a product of old money, Ormesby Hall. This gentle Palladian pile is now oddly situated almost in the middle of a housing estate (just off the B1380, Ladgate Lane), but retains its park and a genteel atmosphere.

The Pennyman family arrived at Ormesby in 1600 in the person of James Pennyman, who probably built the small manor house which was replaced as the main family residence in 1740-5 by Ormesby Hall. The hall was built for the grandson of James Pennyman, but as he died in 1743 much of the work was overseen by his widow, Dorothy. The architect is unknown, but may have been one of Yorkshire's band of gentlemen amateurs, Colonel James Moyser, who was a distant relative of the family and was partly responsible for the design of Nostell Priory in the West Riding.

The three-storey pedimented hall has a fine site looking north towards the Tees, and the interior has much good plasterwork, probably by John Carr. The hall and stables — also attributed to Carr — with the park and the garden together make a complete contrast to industrial Teesside. The Pennymans did not distance themselves from the incomers, being

involved in the expansion of Middlesbrough by building a model village at North Ormesby, on the eastern edge of the town centre, in the 1860s. The Pennyman family lived at the hall until 1983.

The A174 east of Ormesby passes below Eston Nab, a superb viewpoint for those who like their panoramas spiced with the fires of industry. To reach the Nab, take the back road from Ormesby, the B1380, to Normanby and at the main crossroads turn south along West Street and Flatts Lane, crossing the dual carriageway. A variety of footpaths and tracks then lead north-east from the road; the Nab is a mile and a half away, capped by a modern monument, a column erected in 1956. It replaced (and re-used some stone from) a castellated beacon, probably built in 1808 during the war with France, and which had fallen prey to vandals.

A little over a mile north-east of the beacon is the headquarters of its builder, chemicals giant ICI. This is Wilton Castle, standing in a wooded park above the A174 and looking north towards the vast ICI works. The castle, a castellated and symmetrical stone construction, was built about 1807 by the architect of the British Museum, Sir Robert Smirke. It occupies the site of a medieval castle.

Only a mile east is Kirkleatham where Sir William Turner's Hospital, amongst the best of English almshouse buildings, attests to the power of seventeenth and eighteenth century philanthropy. Turner, a successful draper who was twice Lord Mayor of London, founded the hospital in 1668. The hospital building itself, an impressive open quadrangle of almshouses, was erected in 1676 but almost entirely rebuilt in 1741-8.

The northern and southern ranges are two-storey brick structures, but the connecting range is on an altogether larger scale and contains a chapel the size of a church. This is unsurprising as the architect of the chapel was probably James Gibbs, once surveyor to the Commissioners for Building Fifty New Churches in London. Its galleried interior has beautiful carving and wrought ironwork.

Sir William Turner also endowed the Free School; its building of 1709 is now known as the Old Hall. The architect of this solid Queen Anne pile with its grand doorway is unknown, but it was possibly an early work by William Wakefield, the Yorkshire gentleman-architect who designed Duncombe Park, Helmsley. Sir William Turner's childhood home, the Jacobean mansion Kirkleatham Hall, was demolished in 1954-6, although the substantial eighteenth century stable block remains.

The fourth in this most unusual collection of buildings is St Cuthbert's Church, erected around 1760-3 to a design by John Carr, although incorporating part of the tower of a 1731 church. The builder was Redcar master carpenter Robert Corney, who may have made a few changes to the original plan. The overriding impression of this most elegant church is not of Carr's work but of the craggy mausoleum attached to its chancel; this commemoration of Marwood William Turner was designed by James Gibbs and built in 1740. Carr's rebuilding of the church left the octagonal Baroque mausoleum untouched. The plain interior of the mausoleum probably results from an 1839 restoration.

Three miles north of Kirkleatham along the A1042 is Coatham and the coast. Dormanstown, the Dorman Long model town begun in

1918, lies just west of the crossroads before Coatham. The development did not flourish despite involving eminent designers Adshead and Ramsey, and Sir Patrick Abercrombie. Adshead, England's first professor of civic design, also used the neo-Georgian of Dormanstown for the successful Duchy of Cornwall estate in Kennington, south London.

After crossing the A1085 trunk road, a left at the roundabout will eventually lead to a cracking view over Teesmouth from the breakwater at South Gare (the sturdy may walk the three miles along Coatham Sands). The breakwater, two and a half miles in length, was built by the Tees Conservancy Commissioners in 1861-88 to increase the depth of water in the Tees. In this it succeeded, though by only three feet six inches, a small return on such an enterprise. South Gare lighthouse, a cast iron Tuscan column with an octagonal lantern, was built in 1884 by John Fowler, engineer to the commissioners; it rises almost sixty feet above the low-water mark.

Heading back towards Redcar, turn right at the roundabout on the edge of Coatham, then immediately left into Kirkleatham Street, to find the Red Barns Hotel. This is based on Red Barns, a Philip Webb house erected in 1868-70 for Hugh Bell, son of ironmaster Lowthian Bell. Webb designed a very simple house using the local vernacular—brick and pantiles—and extended it in 1875 and 1881-2. It was a significantly unspectacular house for a wealthy man, and as such was influential in architectural circles, with its emphasis on good internal planning and effective functioning.

Coatham was an important medieval port but is now overshadowed by Redcar, into which it merges imperceptibly. In its early days, Redcar was the local resort for Yorkshire gentry who chose not to travel as far as Scarborough. Its population was a little over 1,000 in 1851 and it grew only slowly until the late nineteenth century, when Middlesbrough's boom provided the adjacent urban centre and thus the potential visitors which the resort previously lacked. Redcar's population reached nearly 3,000 in 1881 and shot up to 10,508 in 1911; measured on a percentage basis, by 1911 it had become the twelfth fastest growing resort in England and Wales.

Its success as a resort did not result in an abundance of pleasure buildings, as Redcar tended to attract visitors from a relatively small area and profitability was too low to support large-scale developments.

A pier promotion company was formed in 1866, however, and actually built a pier in 1871-3. It was a jolly and quite elegant affair, with pretty kiosks at the landward end. It suffered damage by shipping and fire on four occasions before 1900, but a pavilion with a ballroom was added in 1907 and the pier lengthened in 1928. This proved to be its heyday; it was breached as a precautionary measure during the Second World War, then further diminished by storms before being demolished in 1980-1.

The seafront is now a rather negative statement, simply the seaward fringe of the town.

One of Redcar's most interesting buildings is the church of St Peter, on Redcar Lane; built by Ignatius Bonomi in 1822-8, its tower boasts a set of four octagonal turrets, complete with battlements. Bonomi's innovative and impressively lofty design was an early example of a Gothic Revival church, a contrast to previous Classical models.

From Redcar, train, beach or the coast road will take you to the miniature resort of Marske-by-the-Sea, where Cliff House, Gothic in style and erected in 1844 as the summer home of the Pease family, overlooks the sea. In the centre of Marske, just off Redcar Road, stands Marske Hall, built around 1620 for Sir William Pennyman and now a Cheshire Home. Its towers, bold bays and lavish fenestration are definitely in the manner of Robert Smythson, who was responsible for the prodigy houses of Longleat and Hardwick Hall, as well as the smaller Fountains Hall in the West Riding. Smythson died in 1614, but his influence lived on as a fashionable building style, popular in the North of England during the 1620s.

Two miles east of Marske is Saltburn, where Pease family influence met the seaside to transform the quiet hamlet of Old Saltburn into the resort of Saltburn-by-the-Sea. Saltburn's growth began in the early seventeenth century, with the discovery of alum-bearing shales in the hills to the south and east of the village. Alum, which had a variety of uses in printing and paper-making amongst others, was obtained from the mined shale by a lengthy process including roasting and adding water. The crystals which eventually resulted were shipped from Saltburn to London. The alum industry, a messy and unpleasant business in its practical details, was of great economic importance in seventeenth century England. At Saltburn, it survived until 1766, when competition forced the local mines to close.

Smuggling partly replaced the lost income from the alum trade during the late eighteenth and early nineteenth centuries, but when Henry Pease first saw Saltburn during the late 1850s it was just a tiny hamlet to the east of Skelton Beck, sheltered by the overbearing form of Hunt Cliff. Henry, brother of Joseph Pease, was a director of the Stockton and Darlington Railway, which at that time was set on expanding its routes towards the coast in order to transport ironstone from the Skelton area. The extension of the railway to Saltburn was something of an afterthought, born of Henry's efforts to emulate Joseph's success in developing Middlesbrough, and also of Henry's travels to the resorts of southern England and the railway towns of North America.

The railway reached little Saltburn on the 17th August 1861; the Saltburn Improvement Company had been established the previous year by the Pease family and various Darlington and Teesside interests. The company bought land for its new resort, on the cliff top west of Skelton Beck, from its owner Lord Zetland and held a competition for a town plan. George Dickinson of Darlington won with a modified grid plan, which had to incorporate the line of the railway track running west to east, effectively dividing the new community in half. The foundation stone of the Zetland Hotel was laid in October 1861 and the resort slowly began to rumble into existence.

The hotel opened in May 1863, pleasure gardens were laid out and a pier followed in 1869. The Improvement Company specified façades in a white brick supplied by the Pease brickworks at Crook in County Durham, which resulted in a happy and doubtless profitable uniformity.

The 'charm bracelet' by Richard Farrington, one of three steel sculptures on Hunt Cliff, near Saltburn. During 1990 the sculptor was in residence at the nearby Skinningrove steelworks, established in 1848.

Until the death of Henry Pease in 1881, development was sedate but well directed; afterwards, economic depression set in and the interests of the Improvement Company were merged with those of the Owners of the Middlesbrough Estate. Although the resort continued to expand its facilities on a small scale, it remained very much a Victorian entity. Without the catchment area required for a mass-market resort, Saltburn veered more towards the residential; in fact, some villas for permanent residents had been present right from the start. Now, Saltburn's picturesque site and refined set of seaside entertainments ensure the resort atmosphere is still maintained.

Any exploration of Saltburn must begin at its birthplace, the railway station, built in 1860-1 and perhaps designed by North Eastern Railway architect Thomas Prosser. (Although it was a Stockton and Darlington station, the two companies were conducting merger negotiations from 1859.) It was a suitably impressive introduction to the resort, with a Classical façade, a large circular booking hall and good ironwork. Not all the original building remains, though it does boast a tiled map showing the North Eastern Railway routes. These maps, which appear in several North-Eastern stations, were produced by tilemakers Craven Dunnill of Jackfield in Shropshire during the early 1900s.

From the station, head north to the sea along any of the jewel streets (Diamond or Ruby, for instance) and on to Marine Parade. Down below is the pier, built in 1868-9 and the first iron pier to be erected on the North-East coast. It was designed by railway contractor John Anderson, Saltburn's resident engineer, and was a 1,400 foot long basic landing stage.

Promenaders did use the pier, however, and the promoting company attempted to raise money by allowing advertisements on the pier. The company was about to press ahead with construction of a pier pavilion

when storms badly damaged the structure in October 1875. Since then the pier has suffered much more damage and undergone rebuilding, resulting today in a 681 foot length with a landward-end pavilion. The pier itself is a surprisingly elegant structure, which fits in

These tile panels, which can be found at Saltburn, Scarborough, Middlesbrough, York and Whitby stations, show the North Eastern Railway network during the early twentieth century. The tiles were manufactured by Craven Dunnill of Shropshire, who specialised in picture panels, often used to decorate pubs in late Victorian and Edwardian times.

well with the delightfully restrained nature of the resort.

Connecting Marine Parade with the promenade is the Cliff Railway, built in 1883-4. It replaced a terrifying hoist which had raised and lowered passengers over the 120 feet of the cliff since 1870. The inclined railway was 207 feet long and worked on the water balance principle, in which water was pumped into a clifftop reservoir and transferred to a tank under the descending car. It was rebuilt in 1921 and still functions, the car taking about twenty seconds to ascend the cliff.

Follow Marine Parade around to the east to find Saltburn's best building — perhaps even Cleveland's best remaining Victorian building — the Zetland Hotel. It was built to the design of William Peachey in 1861-3, and its white-brick Italianate façade is dominated by a central circular tower topped by a telescope room. The hotel was furnished to the highest standards, allowing guests to live in country-house style while enjoying the seaside. The building has now been converted to residential use, losing some of its glamour in the process, but its outward appearance retains the

Saltburn Pier opened in May 1869, and 50,000 people walked its length in the first six months. The promenader paid at an octagonal entry kiosk, and could take refreshment at a centrally placed booth before enjoying the sea air in the saloon at the pierhead.

The cliff railway at Saltburn, which connects the clifftop with the promenade and pier. The railway opened in 1884 and still functions today, although its original gas engines have been replaced by electric motors.

elegance expected of a fashionable resort hotel, with its private, canopied railway platform to the rear.

The Zetland Hotel overlooks both sea and glen, the valley of the Skelton Beck. The glen was bridged in 1868-70 at a point almost half a mile south of the hotel, the bridge standing 120 feet above the lowest point of the valley floor. It was intended to lead to a further development of the resort on the east of the glen, but this was never viable. The pedestrian toll payable to cross the spindly iron structure gave rise to its local name, the Halfpenny Bridge. The bridge was demolished in 1974 due to its deteriorating condition; it cost £50,000 to pull down against an estimated £7,500 to build.

The route of the Cleveland Way footpath between Skelton and the coast passes through part of the glen, under the towering red-brick arches of a handsome railway viaduct, which takes a freight line south-east from Saltburn to the potash mine at Boulby.

Further north, although hidden by trees above the east side of the glen, is the heavily Gothic mansion Rushpool Hall (now an hotel), built for John Bell of the ironfounders firm Bell Brothers in 1862-3. The lavishly-decorated hall was constructed of ironstone and included an underground swimming pool; although most of the interior was lost during a fire on the 20th February 1904, restoration was complete by 1906, and some Moorish plasterwork remains.

Numerous paths through the pretty glen lead to a bridge at the seaward end of the beck, then the Cleveland Way takes to the cliffs, following a well-walked route past the remains of old Saltburn and on to Hunt Cliff, the site of a Roman signal station. The small fort probably dated from the second century and stood near Hunt Cliff's northern extremity, but most of the remains have now been lost to the sea.

The view from the north-facing cliff top is vast; the highest cliff on the east coast of England is only a few miles to the south-east, but the nearest landfall due north is as far away as the Shetland Islands. Beside the cliff path as it heads for the steelworks of Skinningrove are three steel sculptures designed by Richard Farrington in 1990 when he was sculptor in residence at the works. The largest, a giant's charm bracelet, encloses the rural view to the east in a ring of steel, an apt metaphor for the impact of industry on Cleveland.

666 FEET TO THE CAPTAIN'S COLUMN

Whitby and Eskdale

STAND ON top of Rock Cliff and you will find yourself above all else on the eastern edge of England, looking down 666 feet to the sea below. Rock Cliff is the topmost point of Boulby Cliffs, the highest cliffs on England's east coast.

As the path begins to ease down the cliff towards Boulby village, a real architectural oddity appears in a field just to the south, close to Boulby Barns Farm. It is a U-shaped concrete structure, all of seventeen feet in height, with its opening facing out to sea and a concave back wall. The sheep which gently graze around it are unaware of its significance, for this is one of the few remaining elements of Britain's earliest air-raid warning system. It is a Sound Mirror, built in 1916, to assist the defence against zeppelin raids on the nearby Skinningrove steel works. A microphone sited in front of the mirror relayed information to the operator. Even after the invention of radar, sound mirrors were used during the Second World War when interference affected the new early-warning system.

Boulby village itself is half a mile further, and was the site of Cleveland's last functioning alum works. The mineral was first extracted in 1672 and was worked intermittently until closure in 1873. South of the village are the twin chimneys of the huge Boulby potash mine, which, sad to say, is not of tremendous architectural interest, even though it boasts the deepest mine shaft in England at around 4,000 feet.

At Boulby the A174 from Saltburn wriggles near to the coast; on the main road and inland from the cliffs is Loftus, only a mile from the sea but with no aspirations to resort status. Instead, its straggling High Street and market place contain an above-average collection of commercial buildings.

A jolly tower indicates the delicate Gothic town hall, which dates from 1879 and was designed by Edward R Robson. He was once assistant to Newcastle-upon-Tyne's best-known architect, John Dobson, and also to George Gilbert Scott. Robson went on to become the first architect to the London School

Board and published the influential *School Architecture* in 1874.

The main road west of Loftus dips steeply into the wooded valley of Kilton Beck, in which is hidden, about a mile south of the

The Sound Mirror on Boulby Cliffs, built in 1916 as part of the early warning system which predated radar; it comprised a series of concrete mirrors along the coast between Northumberland and Southampton.

road, the substantial ruins of Kilton Castle, dating from the twelfth century.

The castle was partly rebuilt during the thirteenth century, and eventually abandoned in the sixteenth century; even after four centuries of neglect, the roofless, sandstone ruin rises to two stories and still overlooks the deep valley.

A mile and a half south of Loftus on the B1366 (take Station Road from the centre of Loftus) is Liverton, where an apparently Edwardian church hides a stunning Norman chancel arch. The church of St Michael was restored in 1902-3, although large chunks of Norman masonry were included in the rebuilding. The capitals of the chancel arch are alive with activity: a boar is set upon by hounds, while birds, a lion, a dragon and assorted humans are crushed together in curious formation.

Another hidden Norman chancel arch is to be found at All Saints in Easington, just a mile east of Loftus on the main road. Here, too, the church has been rebuilt, in 1888-9 by Charles Hodgson Fowler, architect to the Dean and Chapter of Durham Cathedral and restorer of an enormous number of churches in the North-East. At All Saints, Fowler took the highly-decorative Norman arch and built it into the south wall of the upper floor of the tower.

Two miles south of Easington, along Grinkle Lane, is Grinkle Park, designed in 1882 by Alfred Waterhouse for Jarrow shipbuilder Charles Palmer. Palmer built up a huge Tyneside industrial empire encompassing shipping, coalmining, iron manufacture and shipbuilding during the second half of the nineteenth century. His great innovation in shipbuilding was to see that steam-propelled

The village of of Staithes tumbles towards the small harbour, which is still well used by the local fishing boats or cobles.

iron ships could be profitably used to carry coal. Palmer's Jarrow shipyard launched an iron collier in 1852, and it proved so successful that Palmer set about building a fleet of steam colliers. Palmer acquired his own iron supplies by purchasing ironstone mining rights between Grinkle Park and the coast in the early 1850s.

The ore was initially shipped to Tyneside — where Palmer had four blast furnaces by 1857 — from Port Mulgrave, his own port two miles south-east of Boulby. After 1916 rail transport was used, via an incline connecting mine with railway in the valley of Easington Beck north of Grinkle Park. Palmer's mansion, a castellated Tudor-Gothic pile, was built when

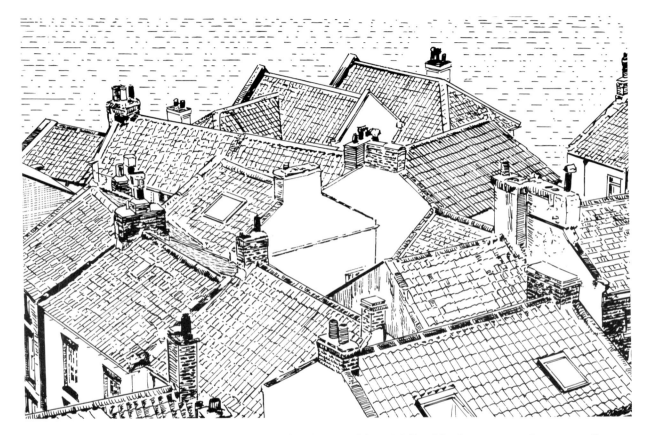

The pantiled roofs of Staithes. Pantiles were first imported from Holland in the seventeenth century, then produced in England from around the start of the eighteenth century. The tiles were particularly fashionable during the Georgian period.

his industrial empire was at its height, but the late 1880s saw a decline which continued until the closure of the Jarrow shipyards in 1934. This was the main event which prompted the Jarrow Crusade of 1936, a 200-strong hunger march from Jarrow to London.

Two miles east of Easington along the A174 is the fishing port (and now tourist haunt) of Staithes, which is completely invisible to the traveller on the main road. The village, a picturesque assembly of tall, pantiled-roofed cottages, clings to the cliff-side around a steep valley about half a mile to the north of the road. Alum and jet mining, smuggling and fishing were important to the growth of the village; when the railway arrived in 1883 enough cod, haddock and mackerel were still being caught to fill three fish trains each week.

The railway line at Staithes was part of the Loftus to Whitby line, the final link on the coastal route between Middlesbrough and Whitby. It was promoted by the Whitby, Redcar and Middlesbrough Union Railway, but the North Eastern had to take the line over

The little village of Staithes, pictured here at dusk, was discovered, in artistic terms, during the 1880s by Gilbert Foster of Leeds, who owned a holiday home at nearby Runswick Bay. Artists from Yorkshire, then further afield, made the village famous as the base of the Staithes Group of painters.

as the original company ran out of funds. The sixteen mile line was expensive at a cost of £42,000, and was the first on the Yorkshire coast to close to passengers, in 1958. Staithes Station brought not only trippers but artists to the previously quiet village; it became artistically fashionable in the 1880s and soon the Staithes Group of painters numbered nearly thirty. Laura Knight is the best known of the group, which flourished until around 1910.

Just a mile east along the coast path is Charles Palmer's Port Mulgrave, founded in the early 1850s as Rosedale Docks, from the Rosedale Cliffs which form the bay. To avoid confusion with Rosedale Abbey near Pickering, the name was changed in 1856. All that remains of the harbour and works are the stone jetties; the tunnel through which Grinkle ironstone arrived at the coast is now sealed.

A day excursion on the train from Middlesbrough to Staithes cost three shillings and two pence in 1925 for a third-class ticket. An extra two pence took the tripper to the next station on the line, Hinderwell, only a mile from the little resort of Runswick Bay. Between Runswick Bay and Whitby the visitor finds a relatively deserted coast; the red-brick cottages at Kettleness were built for railway workers, and a Roman signal station stood half a mile inland.

Coast path and A174 meet at Sandsend, a minor resort created from the two small settlements of Sandsend (to the north), which dates from the thirteenth century, and East Row, which grew up where a pair of becks entered the sea either side of the small cliff known as Sandsend Rigg. The villages were once home to alum miners, but after the arrival

Runswick Bay, where an unusual thatched cottage stands near the end of the sea wall. The village, which is sited on soft shales, had to be rebuilt in 1682 after a landslip.

of the railway, tourism took over and the settlements had merged by the early twentieth century. After closure of the railway the twin viaducts which carried it across the becks were demolished.

A mile to the west of Sandsend is Lythe, where the church of St Oswald dominates the approach to the sea. It was largely built in 1910-11 and is one of the best works of architect Walter Tapper, who learnt his trade from that specialist in Victorian Gothic church building, G F Bodley, and became surveyor to York Minster in 1928. Tapper's early twentieth century churches were often constructed in brick, as funds for ecclesiastical building had become less easily available. The rebuilding of St Oswald cost about £10,000, most of which was provided by a benefaction from one of its churchwardens, the Marquis of Normanby.

The extensive Mulgrave Woods lie to the south of Lythe, enclosing the mainly Norman and thirteenth century remains of old Mulgrave Castle. Its small rectangular keep, probably built in the early fourteenth century, stands between the two becks which flow through the woods into the sea at Sandsend. The castle was partially destroyed after being occupied by royalists during the Civil War.

The new version of Mulgrave Castle is less than half a mile south of Lythe at the woodland's edge. The house was built around 1735 and two wings were added for Lord Mulgrave by Sir John Soane in 1786. Humphry Repton worked on the grounds in 1792-3, developing views of hills and sea.

The castle was remodelled about 1804-11 in a romantic, asymmetrical, castellated style by William Atkinson of Bishop Auckland, who worked for renowned Gothic architect James Wyatt at Auckland Castle around 1795. Atkinson then became a pupil of Wyatt — who was appointed Surveyor of the Office of Works in 1796 — and moved to London. Not only was Atkinson's architectural career successful but he also introduced Atkinson's cement, an external rendering which used raw materials from Lord Mulgrave's estate, to the London market. Mulgrave obtained the post of architect to the Board of Ordnance for Atkinson in 1813.

At low tide, around two miles of beach separates Sandsend and Whitby, but at high tide the walker must brave the A174 until a lane to the east of the golf club house leads towards the cliff top, a first view of the abbey on the far East Cliff and thence into town.

The port and resort of Whitby probably originated as a site for a Roman signal station. The abbey was founded in AD 657, but destroyed by the Danes in the ninth century and not re-founded for two centuries. Abbey and town flourished in medieval times, when the borough was monastic property; this enabled the monks to collect rents, rates and various tolls from the townsfolk.

Whitby Abbey was dissolved in 1539, when the town was still small and crowded around the bottom of East Cliff, between the abbey and the River Esk. A bridge probably existed in 1351, but less development took place on the west side of the river until the town began to grow in the seventeenth and eighteenth centuries, when the shipbuilding industry was in its prime.

Cleveland alum was shipped from Whitby in the seventeenth century, and from the early 1750s whaling ships left for Greenland each summer to catch the Greenland right whale. Its blubber produced oil for lamps and its bones were used in corsets, but replacement of oil by paraffin and eventually gas lamps saw the end of the industry from the 1830s. Fishing and the jet trade were also crucial to Whitby's greatest period of prosperity, between the mid-eighteenth and mid-nineteenth centuries.

Jet, an almost black fossilised wood which occurs in the Jet Rock beds of shale, had been used in jewellery production in the Whitby area from Bronze Age times. Lathe turning was introduced in 1800 (as in amber manufacture), and the industry developed until by 1873 there were 200 jet workshops employing a total of around 1,400 people in Whitby. Whitby jet was given a great boost by the death of Prince Albert, as Queen Victoria wore quantities of black jet jewellery when in mourning. However, fashions changed and by the 1880s the jet industry began its decline.

The growth of Whitby as a seaside resort was initially due to George Hudson, the first railway millionaire, who bought West Cliff Fields in 1848 and began laying out a miniature Brighton on the cliff top. The railway reached Whitby, in the shape of the horse-operated Whitby & Pickering Railway, as early as 1835, but this line only stretched as far as Grosmont, seven miles up the Esk valley. The line, built by George Stephenson, was extended to Pickering the following year and connected into the national system via Malton in 1845, when it was taken over by the York and North Midland Railway. Steam locomotives did not replace the horses until 1847.

The coastal line north from Whitby was opened in 1883 and the Whitby–Scarborough route in 1885. The number of visitors increased apace, but as the town's other industries dwindled, so did the population, from just over 14,000 in 1881 to 11,139 in 1911. Tourism reached its peak in the mid-1930s, when the railway was hard-pressed to cope with the demand. Today the combination of abbey, fishing, shipping and topography make Whitby an attractive working port.

Nowadays fewer travellers arrive at Whitby by rail, but the railway station (partly converted to shops) is still a convenient point from which to set out on an exploration of the town. The station was built in 1847 to the design of George Townsend Andrews, a York architect who was both friend and political associate of George Hudson, the 'Railway King'. Andrews built a fine series of stations on Hudson's lines, mainly in the east of Yorkshire, using variations on a few standard designs. At Whitby he produced an elegant single-storey stone-built structure fronted by an arched *porte cochere*, which sheltered tourists heading for West Cliff.

West Cliff acquired its own station in 1883, the line between the two Whitby stations forming a half mile long U-shape in its descent from cliff top to river.

At the point where it began the turn north into the old town, it was crossed by the spectacular Larpool Viaduct, carrying the Scarborough line across the Esk. Although both West Cliff and Scarborough lines have been closed, the viaduct remains, towering above trains on the Esk Valley route. It was built in 1885 and stands 125 feet above the riverbed; thirteen arches take the track bed the 305 yards across the valley. The gracefulness of the design is emphasised by pairs of arched openings in the base supports of the tallest arches.

Although the main architectural attractions of Whitby lie east of the river, the confused jumble of alleyways, constant changes of level and assortment of pleasant Georgian buildings make the stroll from station to West Cliff enjoyable, and the view from the top is essential. Before beginning the climb, glance west of the station into Bagdale to see Bagdale Old Hall, now an hotel; this L-shaped manor house, built in the 1580s, has mullioned windows and an interior with fine fireplaces, decorated with Dutch and English tiles.

There are many routes to West Cliff; one of the more direct from the station is to head for the river and the swing bridge, which dates from 1909 and is at least the fourth bridge to be built on the site. Here turn into Golden Lion Bank, leading on to Flowergate, and take the first right, Cliff Street. This rises narrow and northward, eventually depositing the walker on East Terrace in New Whitby, as the resort area of the town was originally known.

George Hudson, through his Whitby Building Company, commissioned John Dobson to draw up a plan for the development of West Cliff, which he produced in 1857. By this time Hudson was in serious financial trouble and had left the country. Dobson had previously worked for Hudson in Newcastle-upon-Tyne, providing the basic design for the Central Station around 1848, but was best known for country houses and churches rather than the more lightweight requirements of resort architecture.

His Classical layout of West Cliff resembled a small-scale Georgian Brighton; it involved East Terrace, which overlooks river and abbey and was built from around 1850, and the fine four-storey Royal Crescent which faces the sea. The crescent, only partially completed, was the centrepiece of Dobson's plan. When Hudson ceased to fund building on West Cliff, development was continued by Sir George Elliott.

At the north end of East Terrace is the famous whale jawbone arch celebrating the whaling industry; the spot also marks a splendid viewpoint and heralds the down-ward path to the Khyber Pass, a road cut through rock to connect West Cliff with Pier Road near sea level. A tiny tunnel in the embankment offers an even quicker route to the quayside, emerging near the West Pier.

The pier was built in the early nineteenth century by the Whitby Harbour engineer, Jonathan Pickernell, who was appointed to his the post in 1781 after working as surveyor of bridges for the County of Northumberland. The seventy foot high lighthouse — a fluted column topped by an octagonal lantern — towards the pier end was erected in 1831 by Francis Pickernell, Whitby Harbour engineer from 1822 and probably grandson of Jonathan.

Unless the end of the pier beckons, press on past the arcades of Pier Road and back towards the swing bridge; once across on the east side, head left down Sandgate to Market Place, dominated by the town hall which dates from 1788. This, too, was designed by Jonathan Pickernell and is of the hall-above-open-arcade variety, although here the architect introduced a central stone drum containing the stairs to the upper floor.

Church Street, at the far end of Market Place, leads inexorably to the 199 steps of Church Stairs, passing several good shop

Climbing the Church Stairs at Whitby. The 199 steps lead to the parish church on top of East Cliff.

Around five million bricks went into the construction of the Larpool Viaduct, near Whitby, in 1885. It took the now-disused Scarborough line across the Esk Valley.

St Mary, the parish church of Whitby, is crammed with galleries and box pews into which a congregation of 2,000 could be squeezed.

Whitby harbour, with the abbey, parish church and Abbey House in the distance on East Cliff.

West Cliff, Whitby, seen from across the River Esk. This elegant development was initiated by George Hudson in the 1850s, but was never completed.

fronts on the way (including the tiled façade of the jet shop). Beside the steps, which date from 1370, is Donkey Road, a cobbled road which was once the main route out of Whitby past the abbey. Look back from the steps for stunning views across the Esk to West Cliff, over red-pantiled cottages and colourful fishing boats down below in the harbour.

St Mary's Church, the parish church of Whitby, stands in its churchyard at the head of the stairs. The exterior with its stubby tower is part Norman and part later medieval, but to a large extent is the result of Georgian alterations. The interior is also a mixture of styles and dates, but the first impression is wholly and wonderfully Georgian. It is packed to its gallery with box pews, and a particularly splendid example in white cuts dramatically across the line of the Norman chancel arch. This is the pew of the Cholmley family, lords of the manor, and dates from the late seventeenth century. It was built in the form of a small gallery supported on twisting barley-sugar columns.

This is all perfectly theatrical, and the effect is heightened by the three-decker pulpit of 1778. It originally took centre stage in front of the Cholmley pew. This dominance of congregation by pulpit was common during the eighteenth century, and the arrangement of pews at St Mary shows what a Georgian worshipper would have found in a typical town church.

Whitby Abbey, the culmination of any visit to Whitby, is almost on the doorstep of the church. It was founded by St Hilda of Hartlepool at the request of King Oswy of Northumbria in AD 657, in celebration of Oswy's victory over Penda of Mercia two years before. In AD 664 the monastery hosted the crucial Synod of Whitby, which set the course of Christian religion in Britain on Roman rather than Celtic lines. However, in AD 867 the abbey was destroyed by the Danes, and not refounded until around 1078 when monks from Evesham in Worcestershire settled at the site.

The wealth of the new abbey grew rapidly in the twelfth century to make it the third richest Benedictine house in Yorkshire. Its church was rebuilt in the first half of the thirteenth century and completed in the fourteenth century, but the number of monks began to decline from the forty or so of the late twelfth century until by the Dissolution there were only twenty-two remaining.

The abbey was then leased to the Cholmley family and was in their hands until 1791. Inevitably the church was used as a source of building materials, but perhaps because it served as a marker for sailors it was not completely destroyed. But the nave fell in 1762, the central tower collapsed in 1830 and the remains suffered from German shelling in 1914.

Today the most striking part of the ruined abbey church is the north wall of the north transept which still stands to its full height, but it is the nature of the surroundings, so unlike many other monastic sites in peaceful valleys, which makes Whitby memorable.

Little of the monastic buildings survive; the masonry was probably used to construct Abbey House, south-west of the church. It was built by Francis Cholmley around 1583-93 and remodelled in 1633-6. Sir Hugh Cholmley added a banqueting hall in 1672-82, a time when pleasure buildings were coming into fashion, and the two storey, eleven bay façade of the sizeable hall now looks towards the abbey. Abbey House has been much altered since the seventeenth century, but the mere fact that it remains, so close to both abbey and parish church, serves to remind us of the nature of power in late medieval times.

The River Esk, which divides the town of Whitby but provides it with such splendid views, rises near Esklets at the head of Westerdale. Around thirty miles of river separate Esklets from the coast, and the gentle valley of Eskdale may be explored by train as far west as Castleton (where the Esk turns south into Westerdale), or by road to within a couple of miles of Esklets, but even more thoroughly on foot.

The first settlement upstream from Whitby is Ruswarp, where both road and rails cross the Esk, and the mill, built in 1752 for Nathaniel Cholmley, stands beside the river. The B1416, which leaves Whitby at its western edge, here heads south to Sneaton where a right turn into a by-road will bring the traveller to a junction just north of Ugglebarnby. The rich interior of All Saints Church, built in the tiny settlement in 1872, is alive with angels, ornamenting the hammerbeam roof and flying out from the font cover. The medieval church on the same site was demolished around 1700; its plain Georgian replacement was in need of restoration by the 1860s, and the new church was funded by subscription, with the highly-decorative interior provided by the Allan family, local shipowners.

Ugglebarnby Church is one of several in and around Eskdale to be rebuilt in the Victorian period, when a new and narrow vision of acceptable styles for church architecture was being propounded. Without the possibility of financial security provided by benefactions, much less rebuilding would have taken place; the combination of fashion, religion and ready money not surprisingly proved powerful, and hastened the end of some early but still-serviceable churches.

Eight miles west of Ugglebarnby is Grosmont, perched on the north bank of the River Murk Esk just to the south of the Esk's main stream. Here the Esk Valley and Pickering railway lines diverge, and the North Yorkshire Moors Railway, which has run the Grosmont to Pickering section since 1967, has its northern depot. Beside the tunnel which takes the steam trains out of Grosmont is the castellated entrance to a diminutive tunnel, now occupied by a footpath. This was the original tunnel used by Stephenson's horse-drawn railway, and is only ten feet wide and fourteen feet high. It was built in 1836 and its replacement opened in 1847.

A path to the east of the tunnel leads to the church of St Matthew, happily sited above a meander of the Murk Esk. The church was rebuilt in 1875-84 when Grosmont was something of an ironstone mining boom-town; rich deposits were discovered nearby in 1839, but the local furnaces shut in 1891 due to competition from imported iron.

A long mile west of Grosmont is Egton Bridge; rails, river and road connect the two, but best is the footpath (left off the Egton road soon after crossing the Esk) which takes the walker past a toll house complete with charge board on its way through the Egton Manor Estate.

The hefty Roman Catholic church of St Hedda is an unexpected find in the pretty

The heavily-weathered sandstone ruins of Whitby Abbey, on its magnificent site above the mouth of the River Esk.

Whitby Abbey at sunset.

little village. It was built in 1866-7, and boasts unusual decoration inside and out. There are coloured relief panels on the exterior walls, while inside are paintings and an ornate altar. The Egton area was for long a Catholic stronghold; Nicholas Postgate, the last English martyr, lived close by. He was hanged in 1679.

West of Egton Bridge, a beautiful series of rolling dales run south from Eskdale; first Glaisdale, then Great and Little Fryup Dales, and Danby Dale, with the village of Danby at its northern extremity. Overlooking Danby from the ridge separating Little Fryup and Danby Dales is the ruin of Danby Castle, a small palace-cum-fortress of fourteenth century construction which is now a farmhouse.

Danby Church is situated well out of the village, about two miles up Danby Dale, in a convenient position for members of the congregation who lived in scattered dale-side farms. Its architectural history, ranging from Norman details to Edwardian alterations, is less impressive than its moorland site and its association with Canon John Christopher

The church of St Matthew at Grosmont was rebuilt in 1875-84. Its east window was part of the previous church, which was erected in 1841-50.

Atkinson. The noted antiquarian and naturalist was Vicar of Danby for fifty-three years, between 1847 and his death in 1900. His classic account of moorland life, *Forty Years in a Moorland Parish*, was published in 1891. He is buried in Danby churchyard.

At Castleton, just over a mile west of Danby, railway and river part company. The source of the Esk lies five miles to the south-west in Westerdale, while the route of the railway runs west towards the Cleveland escarpment, descending into the vale at Battersby. The minor road which takes the driver out of the moors via Commondale and Kildale follows much the same route, arriving in the vale at Easby, about a mile north-west of Battersby. In the grounds of early nineteenth century Easby Hall, just to the north of the road from the moors, is a private chapel dating from 1882 and beside it an ornate mausoleum with an octagonal pyramid roof.

Overlooking Easby from the moor to the east is the substantial obelisk of Captain Cook's Monument. Several tracks criss-cross Easby Moor and pass the monument, but the easiest to follow is probably the section of the Cleveland Way which begins at Kildale.

The monument was built in 1827-8 by Whitby financier Robert Campion in memory of one of Cleveland's favourite sons. James Cook was born in 1728 in Marton, now a southern suburb of Middlesbrough, and went to school in Great Ayton, only a couple of miles to the west of the monument. He worked in Staithes, then moved to Whitby before going to sea in 1747 and emerging as a great explorer and navigator; he was killed in Hawaii during an expedition in 1779.

Cook's monument is a hefty stone obelisk fifty-one feet in height; the captain's career is described on plaques mounted at its base. Its solidity and landlocked setting make it a strange monument for a sailor, but maybe the bleak and windswept moors hark back to the desperate dangers of an explorer's life.

CRESCENT AND CELL,
RESORT AND RELIGION
The North York Moors

IF THE development plans of the Peak Estate Company had succeeded, walkers ambling through peaceful Ravenscar today would have been greeted by the noise and activity of a Blackpool or a Scarborough, for Ravenscar is the resort which never was.

The cliff-top site went against it from the start in 1895, when the new company's backers saw fit to ignore the difficulty of descending 600 feet to the shore, which in any case was provided with rocks rather than sand. But the company pressed ahead, building roads and laying on drainage and mains water; there was a railway station, and also an esplanade and a crescent, necessities for a proper resort, but buyers of building plots were few in number. By 1913, most of the 1,500-odd plots remained unsold and the company was wound up.

An hotel was erected and a links golf course laid out on land to the west of the incipient resort, but little else happened and nature slowly reclaimed the roads, though odd sections still show through the grass. The notion of a resort at such an unpropitious location seems peculiar now, but would have seemed less so in the late nineteenth century, when the business of providing seaside entertainment offered the prospect of almost instant wealth.

Many were the companies which set up at that time to build everything from entire resorts to copies of the Eiffel Tower, and some proved to be lasting successes, although of course there were numerous financial disasters, and even a few frauds and deceptions.

Ravenscar's name began with the failed resort, but its history did not, for even in 1650 alum was being mined in the area which was then known as the Peak, after Old Peak Cliff at the southern end of Robin Hood's Bay. The remains of the Peak Alum Works can be found just west of Ravenscar, off the Cleveland Way; the ruins of its well-formed stone walls were passed off as the masonry of an ancient abbey by the desperate (or perhaps just misinformed) Peak Estate Company. The

Looking towards Ravenscar, the site of an unsuccessful resort development at the end of the nineteenth century, from Robin Hood's Bay.

works — closed in 1862 — employed over 100 workers at its height.

The great attraction of Ravenscar today is the view over Robin Hood's Bay to the north; to reach the village itself, the walker may follow either the Cleveland Way along the coast or the course of the old railway line further inland. Drivers must return to the A171 and head north, with good views over coast and moorland, before turning back towards the sea nearly a mile north of the B1416 intersection. This by-road leads over Brow Top, where the bay becomes visible once more, and passes close to Fyling Hall before dropping down towards Fylingthorpe and Robin Hood's Bay.

Fyling Hall was built soon after 1819 for Whitby shipbuilder and owner John Barry. It is a pleasant enough house with a fine sea view, but its main attraction lies in the nearby pigsty, erected around 1883 for John Warren Barry, who owned the hall from 1871.

It is a pigsty fit for the gods of the porcine world, a Classical temple on a human scale decorated with Egyptian detailing. The six Egyptianised Ionic columns supporting the pediment are constucted of timber, making both purpose and structure of the sty impossible to define at first glance. Barry's grand tour of southern Europe must have been the source of inspiration for this swineish ideal home, which took over three years to build, as a result of its owner's constant changes of mind regarding the design. Recently the sty, intended for just a pair of happy porkers, has undergone minimal alterations to allow it to function as a holiday home for human tenants.

The nondescript outskirts of Robin Hood's Bay sprawl a little over the cliff top, but the picturesque heart of the village is jammed into a narrow cleft in the rocks, its main street winding steeply down towards the sea through a jumble of pantiled-roofed cottages and shops.

The village, known as Bay or Bay Town, originated in the early sixteenth century and prospered through fishing and merchant shipping. By the nineteenth century it supported over 130 fishermen and all their associated workers. When the railway arrived in 1885 the Mount Pleasant residential area was developed on the cliff top, but already the fishing trade was declining due to the constraints of the harbour. Now its wayward appeal brings tourists by the coachload, but its vertiginous alleys and numerous changes of level swallow up school parties and rucksacked walkers alike.

No single structure stands out, but the overall effect of buildings and bay is stunning, especially in the early morning light. There are few modern intrusions, but the early twentieth century green ceramic façade of Bay Fisheries is a notable exception. Relief tiles of sheep and cow heads on the frieze show that this was originally a butcher's shop.

Heading north out of Robin Hood's Bay, the traveller will come upon St Stephen Old Church, situated high above the bay on the B1447 almost a mile out of the village. It was built in 1821-2, replacing an older structure on the site, and itself was replaced as the parish church of Fylingdales in 1868-70 when St Stephen New Church was erected back in the village.

The old church retains its galleries, box pews and a three-decker pulpit, all contained by a severe stone exterior. The sea is all-pervading; not only is there a wonderful view of the bay but memorials to the shipwrecked can be found in church and churchyard.

The road from the bay crosses the main A171 at Hawsker, continuing west via Sneatonthorpe to the B1416; a choice of by-roads then takes the traveller down into the valley of Little Beck, a tributary of the Esk, which is straddled by the tiny and perfect hamlet of Littlebeck. Here amblers may follow Little Beck south through woodland to Falling Foss, a thirty foot waterfall.

Hidden away in the woods is the Hermitage, a sizeable room hollowed out of a huge boulder, which stands above the east bank of the beck about half a mile south of the hamlet. It was intended not for a hermit but as a shelter; the seats inside can accommodate about twenty people. It bears the date 1790 and the initials GC, which are believed to refer to George Chubb, a local schoolmaster involved in building the nearby shooting lodge Newton House (now a field centre). Despite the obvious difficulties of undertaking the construction of this shelter in the eighteenth century, the Hermitage is a strangely disappointing folly.

Climb out of the valley and turn south on the A169; after almost two miles, take the Goathland turning to the right. The moor top gives a good view to the west as the road crosses the whinstone ridge, a basalt intrusion which runs in a straight line north-west to south-east between Eskdale and Fylingdales Moor. The road then descends another mile or so into Goathland.

This attractive village is spread out around a large open common, from which a path leads north to the Mallyan Spout waterfall on West Beck. West Beck and Eller Beck meet at Beck Hole, a mile north-west of Goathland, to form the Murk Esk. There are numerous waterfalls in these parts; Nelly Ayre Foss is a mile upstream from the Spout, while Thomason Foss is just upstream from Beck Hole on Eller Beck.

The proximity of gorges, fast-flowing streams and waterfalls led to Goathland becoming a fashionable haunt for the more discerning type of tripper in Victorian times. It has almost the air of a spa town, albeit on a small scale, and in the nineteenth century could provide suitably thrilling, even sublime, natural diversions combined with comfortable accommodation. These things it continues to do today.

A bridlepath leads from the common at Goathland towards Wade's Causeway, an excavated mile-long section of the Roman Wheeldale Road. The bridlepath runs south-west then south, meeting the splendid stonework of the roadway about two miles from Goathland. Access for drivers is also possible using the narrow moorland road from Egton Bridge to Pickering. Take the road west out of Goathland, soon bearing right at a junction; at the crossroads in two and a half miles, turn left to join the route to Wade's Causeway. The road peters out into a rough track as it reaches the Roman road.

The Wheeldale Road was part of the Roman road connecting Malton and Pickering, to the south, with a signal station at Kettleness on Runswick Bay, about six miles north-west of Whitby. Tracks followed most of the main moorland ridges before Roman times. From at least the thirteenth century, some of these causeways were paved with local flagstones by people of the moorland villages, to ensure good conditions for pack ponies. Remnants of these paved tracks, which became crucial to trade in the seventeenth century, can be seen throughout the moors, but particularly in Eskdale. The Roman roads were never paved, and at Wheeldale the upper gravel surface of the road has been weathered away, leaving hardcore stone slabs and drainage ditches clearly visible. Wade's Causeway marches steadily onward, a small part of imperial Roman power civilising the isolated and inhospitable territory of Wheeldale Moor.

The Roman road is one of the oldest landmarks on the North York Moors, and has certainly survived longer than the nearby triumvirate dating from 1964 which became one of the great sights of the area, the three huge white golf balls of Fylingdales Early Warning Station. Each 116 foot high geodesic dome, a theoretically demountable greenhouse-style structure made up of 1,300 plastic panels, sat on a massive concrete foundation block, and sheltered a radar dish which kept watch to the north and east during the Cold War years. The redundant radomes were demolished in 1993, leaving just their modern counterpart, a hulking pyramid which scans the world for incipient dangers. Public perception of the golf balls changed from initial horror to something resembling affection; the best-selling postcard of the moors featured the homely domes. Doubtless we shall all grow to love their toaster-shaped replacement.

For a view of this rather inelegant structure, take the train south or head back to the A169 via the road south from the church on Goathland Common, and turn right on to the main road. Around two miles out of Goathland, nearing Eller Beck Bridge, the pyramid comes into view to the east. For a closer look, head east on the moorland path at Eller Beck Bridge.

South of Fylingdales, road and rail head towards the woodlands which mark the southern slope of the moors, actually the Tabular Hills.

The train stops at Levisham Station, a mile or so walk from the village itself, which is a mile west of the A169, through Lockton. The church of St Mary, with its Saxon chancel arch, is not in Levisham village but down by the delightful Levisham Beck and only accessible along a narrow track, which leads south off the Lockton road.

At the head of the beck, about two miles north of Levisham along a waterside path, is the Hole of Horcum, a natural amphitheatre which is the largest hollow in Yorkshire. The A169 overlooks the Hole, about three miles south of Eller Beck Bridge. The Hole is said to have been carved out by either the Devil or the giant known as Wade, legendary builder of the eponymous causeway, but the more mundane explanation is that it was created by a combination of glaciers and springs. It is now meadowland.

Across Newton Dale from Levisham is Newton-on-Rawcliffe, and a by-road which leads west via the villages of the southern moorland slopes; such is the depth of the dale that there is no road crossing other than near Goathland, and drivers must travel down to Pickering before turning back and heading north through Newbridge to Newton, just on the far side of the railway track from Levisham Station. The route west from Newton to Cawthorne passes the sites of four Roman camps on the hillside to its west, just where the road turns sharply south. At Cropton the motte and bailey castle has a fine view up into Rosedale; bear right here, and right again at the next junction to head north into Rosedale.

The village of Rosedale Abbey is five miles to the north, idyllic in winter but overcrowded in summer. All that remains of the Cistercian nunnery which gave the village its name is a single, undistinguished pillar of masonry. The nunnery was founded in the mid-twelfth century, and although overrun by the Scots in 1322, it survived until 1538. The church of St Mary and St Lawrence dates from 1839-40, and was designed by the eclectic and successful London architect Lewis Vulliamy. Its lectern, perhaps seventeenth century Dutch, is held aloft by an angel.

Much of the village housing is gently Gothic in style, clearly part of a planned development. The reason for both housing and church is the presence of ironstone.

There was probably an ironworks in Rosedale in medieval times, but the remoteness of the dale, combined with a lack of high-quality ore which could be worked using contemporary technology, meant that serious exploitation only began about 1836. Then Rosedale became an industrial boom-town, with railway tracks, kilns, mines, chimneys and waste heaps all around. The Rosedale Ironstone Railway, which connected the dale with the main line on the northern edge of the moors fourteen miles away at Battersby, was opened in 1861.

As ever, boom turned to bust and high-quality foreign ore ousted Rosedale's production; the Ironstone Railway closed in 1929, and after almost a century of hectic industrial activity, peace returned to the dale. Ironstone mining has left Rosedale with a legacy of industrial detritus: kilns, disused railway tracks and other reminders of the past now do sterling service as tourist attractions.

The steep Hutton-le-Hole by-road leading south out of the village soon brings the walker to Bank Top and a set of tall masonry arches. These are the ironstone calcining kilns in which ore was roasted to drive out water and reduce its weight prior to transportation. The mine, a source of magnetic ironstone, lay to the south of the road and was worked by the Rosedale and Ferryhill Iron Company from 1856. Before the coming of the railway the ore was taken to Pickering by packhorse, whence it travelled by rail via York to the company's main furnaces in County Durham.

The village of Lastingham is four miles almost directly south of Rosedale Abbey, but road access is only via Hutton-le-Hole or Cropton. The great delight of this little village — really no more than a couple of streets of houses — is the surprise which awaits beneath the church of St Mary. Here is a crypt which is a perfectly-preserved eleventh century church, complete with nave, aisles and an apsidal chancel all defined by hugely massive columns.

This inspirational structure came about after a monastery was founded at Lastingham by St Cedd in AD 654. Danish destruction intervened before the monastery rose again in 1078, when monks from Whitby began to build a church, which must almost have been finished when the monks abandoned the site and moved on to York in 1085. The crypt (actually a shrine to St Cedd) and part of the east end of the church above ground date from this period of building, although towards its west end the church dates from the thirteenth century, and the tower is fifteenth century. All was sympathetically restored in 1879 by John Loughborough Pearson. But it is the unique crypt which remains in the memory, with its lowering roof, monastic apse and powerful masonry.

Just over a mile south of Lastingham, along Oldfield Lane, is the pretty village of Appleton-le-Moors, with its two rows of cottages neatly arranged either side of a single main street. The back gardens, generally regular strips of land, are hemmed in by a pair of parallel back lanes. Although the houses are by no means of similar ages, they adhere to the ancient property line with respect to the road. This geometric layout did not arise purely by chance. Far from being a product of irregular village growth, Appleton is indeed a planned settlement, dating from the reconstruction of local villages following devastation by the Normans and Danes in 1069-70. Appleton is one amongst many planned villages, but has retained its original form more than most.

Just over two miles north-west of Appleton is the charming village of Hutton-le-Hole, at its best in the winter months when the press of visitors diminishes and an array of cottages can be seen dotted around the valley, divided by Hutton Beck which tumbles its way through the rural scene. The village was mentioned in the *Domesday* survey, and survived on a mix of small-scale coalmining and ironstone working, carried out in the dales to the north-west, and linen weaving.

Peaceful Farndale lies to the north of Hutton; take the road north to Blakey Ridge, then bear left into the valley after a mile, along Dale End Road. About four miles into the dale, east of its river, the Dove, is the hamlet of Church Houses and its church, St Mary.

This high moorland church was built in 1831 but much changed in 1907-14 by Temple Moore, one-time assistant to George Gilbert Scott junior. Moore specialised in Gothic churches, and often worked in the industrial towns of the North, as well as the less populous countryside of the North and East Ridings. In 1908 he was also working at Gillamoor, a couple of miles west of Hutton in lower Farndale, where he re-furnished the church of St Aidan.

Around nine miles west of Hutton lies Ryedale, which encloses within its steepling vale a jewel of the English Picturesque — the hamlet of Rievaulx, with its abbey and terrace above.

Only at Fountains can it be said that there are more substantial and impressive monastic remains than at Rievaulx Abbey, but the Ryedale site, despite also playing its role in eighteenth century landscape gardening, has an air of wildness that the lawns of Studley Royal surely lack.

The Cistercian abbey of Rievaulx was founded in 1132 by the white monks of Clairvaux, who settled on land given by Walter l'Espec, lord of Helmsley, in the previous year.

The abbey was an instant success, attracting 300 monks and lay brothers within its first ten years; by the 1160s there were 140 monks and 500 to 600 lay brothers.

The puritanical and efficient Cistercians built mightily at Rievaulx, dealing with the unhelpful westward-sloping location by setting the liturgical east of their abbey at the south end of the site. The plain and severely Romanesque nave dates from the earliest period of building, 1135-40, and makes a tremendous contrast with the Gothic of the magnificent chancel, built around 1230, by which time the wealth of the Cistercians had not surprisingly fostered changes in their way of life, including their attitude to architectural ornament. The church, which is all of 370 feet in length, was largely floored by a tile pavement, some fragments of which may still be seen.

The construction of such a splendid church and the equally fine monastic buildings left the monks heavily in debt, and from around 1300 the fortunes of Rievaulx went into a

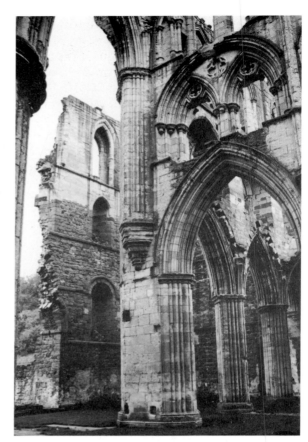

*The interior of the church at Rievaulx Abbey, look-
ing towards the chancel, which was built around
1230. The chancel arch, topped by two small
windows, reaches seventy-five feet in height.*

*Inside the church at Rievaulx Abbey, where the north
transept and chancel meet under the soaring
chancel arch.*

decline which was furthered by the Black
Death. Some of the ancilliary buildings were
demolished even before the Dissolution as
they had become surplus to requirements.
The monastery was dissolved in 1538, when
only the abbot and twenty-one monks

remained, and after changing hands several
times the site was bought by London banker
Sir Charles Duncombe in 1687. Fortunately,
although a blast-furnace complex was created
at Rievaulx by its late sixteenth century owners,
so little interest was taken in the fabric of the

abbey that its stone had not even been removed for building purposes.

Much the most romantic view of the abbey may be obtained from Ashberry Hill, on the far side of the Rye valley. Cross the Rye at Rievaulx Bridge, half a mile south of the abbey (look out for the splendid garden beside the bridge), and follow the road a little way west to Ashberry Farm. Take the footpath which disappears behind the farm and wends its way around the flank of Ashberry Hill, directly west of the abbey. As the path rises, the ruins — and the terrace above — may be glimpsed through the trees; the view is all the better in winter, of course.

The abbey became involved in the evolution of English Picturesque taste after the death of Sir Charles Duncombe in 1711. Duncombe's

The signpost at Ashberry Farm, Rievaulx, is a reminder of the administrative past.

Yorkshire estates were inherited by his brother-in-law, Thomas Brown, who changed his name to Duncombe and immediately began to build a house to the south-west of Helmsley, which he called Duncombe Park. A long, curving terrace with a small Classical temple at either end was laid out beside the house, overlooking the Rye. Thomas Duncombe I was succeeded by his son Thomas, who died in 1746, leaving the property to his son Thomas Duncombe III. Probably inspired by the example of the Aislabie landscape garden at Studley Royal, which used Fountains Abbey as the ultimate Picturesque eyecatcher, Thomas III began work on plans to connect the Duncombe terrace with a new terrace at Rievaulx.

He built Rievaulx Terrace above the abbey around 1751-61, adding the rectangular Ionic temple at the north end and the circular Tuscan temple at the Duncombe end, both around 1758. It seems he intended to connect the two terraces using a viaduct to cross the steep valley just to the south of the abbey; thus carriages would have been able to drive along the ridge between Duncombe and Rievaulx, the series of superlative views ending with the wonderful Gothic set-piece of the abbey.

Sadly the viaduct was never built, but visitors may now enjoy the views from the half mile of Rievaulx Terrace; access is from the B1257, where the road north out of Rievaulx climbs to the top of the valley.

Both the Rievaulx temples were probably designed by Sir Thomas Robinson of Rokeby Hall, one of the best of Yorkshire's amateur architects. Robinson was always at the height of fashion, and his expensive passions for building and entertaining eventually led to

The Picturesque landscape: Rievaulx Abbey seen from the Ionic temple, built around 1758 on Rievaulx Terrace by Thomas Duncombe III.

the enforced sale of his family home. At Rievaulx, the interior of his Ionic temple was sumptuously fitted out for use as a banqueting hall, with a painted ceiling, high-quality wood carving and a white marble chimney-piece. The interior of the smaller Tuscan temple is floored with medieval tiles taken either from the abbey below or from nearby Byland Abbey.

More medieval tiles may be found at the church of All Saints in the isolated hamlet of Old Byland, two miles west of Rievaulx by way of the road to Rievaulx Bridge; turn right at the bridge, then again shortly at the farm. All Saints, hidden behind cottages, is small but unusual, with fragments of horse-faced Norman dragons ornamenting the exterior of the porch. The medieval tiled altar pavement is a rarity in Yorkshire.

In 1143 Old Byland was briefly colonised by monks from Furness Abbey before they moved on to found Byland Abbey, four miles to the south. The proximity of Rievaulx and Old Byland had proved too much for the monks at the smaller foundation, who could hear the bells of Rievaulx at all hours.

From Rievaulx, the road north through Ryedale leads into the wide, green valley of Bilsdale, and climbs to its highest point on the northern edge of the moors. Here, from the car park near the brow at Clay Bank Top, wonderfully expansive views of Cleveland and the moors to the east may be seen. Just over four miles away and almost directly north is Captain Cook's Monument on Easby Moor, while to the east is Greenhow Bank, scaled by the course of the Rosedale Ironstone Railway incline with a gradient of one in five at its steepest. Here wagonloads of ironstone were let down by cable towards the junction at Battersby, simultaneously hauling empty wagons up the slope by force of gravity.

At Ingleby Greenhow, a couple of miles to the north (take the road which leaves the B1257 beside the Clay Bank Top car park), is the church of St Andrew with its confusing but jolly stone carvings of a pig, a bear and other animals. The church is basically Norman

The ruins of Rievaulx Abbey, seen from an excellent viewpoint to the west, the footpath on Ashberry Hill.

but was thoroughly rebuilt in 1741; the odd carvings ornament the capitals of the north arcade, and are perhaps vernacular nineteenth century additions.

West of Ingleby Greenhow, a succession of small villages rings the north face of the Cleveland Hills. In the back lanes of Great Broughton, the first village to be met by those descending the road from Clay Bank Top, a beck runs under a series of tiny bridges connecting cottages with the main street. Half a mile west at Kirkby-in-Cleveland, the church of St Augustine offers two buildings in one: an entire Georgian structure dating from 1815,

The Ionic temple — a banqueting hall — adorns Rievaulx Terrace, created around 1751-61 by Thomas Duncombe III, who turned part of Ryedale into a magnificent landscape garden.

with the early twentieth century addition of a chancel by the ubiquitous Temple Moore.

Three miles further on in Carlton-in-Cleveland, just off the A172 south of Stokesley, is yet another Temple Moore church, St Botolph, which was erected in 1896-7. It was the second new church to be built in the parish inside two decades. Vicar George Sangar had

completed the previous church in 1879, but it was burnt down three years later and Sangar was charged with arson, though later cleared of the crime. Foxhunting man and publican J L Kyle replaced Sangar as the incumbent in 1894, and set about raising the necessary funds for rebuilding. The new St Botolph, where Kyle remained until his death in 1943, is neo-

Gothic and has an elegant lychgate, also designed by Moore. Carlton's manor house, a small-scale Palladian affair of 1740-50, stands right on the village street in curious juxtaposition with the cottages.

Travelling south-west along the A172 we pass Whorl Hill, reputedly the lair of a dragon, and Whorlton-in-Cleveland, a hamlet with little else but a ruined Norman church and the remains of a castle. This odd hamlet can easily be reached on foot from Carlton.

Further west, where the face of the hills turns to look west, the A172 bypasses Ingleby Arncliffe, leaving Arncliffe Hall above and to the east. The hall was built by John Carr around 1750-4 for Thomas Mauleverer, and contains some tremendous Rococo plaster-work. The west-facing rear of Carr's otherwise typically Palladian design has a weird venetian window in which the central light is blank. The church of All Saints stands in the churchyard just below the hall. It was rebuilt in 1821 on the site of a Norman predecessor. Inside there are box pews.

Not far south of Ingleby Arncliffe, where A172 and A19 meet in a flurry of rowdy traffic, is the Cleveland Tontine Inn, built from 1804 for the use of traffic on the Yarm to Thirsk turnpike road. A tontine was a means of raising a loan for building whereby the original loan was paid back in annuities, the amount rising as the eventual death of individual subscribers diminished the number eligible for payment. The capacious and rather Gothic stables were added in 1806 when mail coaches were introduced on the Sunderland to Boroughbridge route. Happily the Tontine still retains its original function as an inn and now restaurant.

The scarp of the Hambleton Hills runs south from the Tontine, hiding on its wooded slope a few surprises, the first of which is almost immediately to the south of the inn, just east of the A19. A great cloister ringed with what appear to be tiny cottages marks out Mount Grace Priory, the home of Carthusian monks from 1398 and the best-preserved charterhouse in England. The Carthusians lived as did ancient Egyptian hermits, generally keeping to a vow of silence and occupying themselves with reading, prayer and manual labour in their individual cells. Lay brothers looked after buildings and farmsteads, and the monasteries or charterhouses remained small in size, enabling the monks to keep strictly to their original principles and escape worldly corruption.

The Carthusians were criticised by members of other orders for their unworldliness, but the continued purity of the order in England led to their popularity in royal circles in the fourteenth century, and Carthusian foundations were still being created long after those of rival orders.

Mount Grace was founded by Thomas de Holand, a nephew and favourite of Richard II who was executed in 1400 for conspiring against Henry IV. Long arguments resulted over ownership of their lands, but despite this the Carthusians built most of the charterhouse at Mount Grace within a few years of its establishment.

The great quadrangular cloister hid twenty-one separate two-storey cells, each with its food hatch next to the doorway, although the design made it impossible for the monk to communicate with the bringer of food. The accommodation was almost luxurious for the time, with piped water, a fireplace, garderobe and garden, but silence was the price of this privacy.

Much of the cloister is still visible, as well as the church to the south and guest house to the west. With its beautiful, verdant setting in the lee of the hills, Mount Grace is humbling and awe-inspiring, in many ways the most memorable monastic site in England.

On the bank above Mount Grace, attainable via a footpath south from the monastic site, is the Lady Chapel, built early in the sixteenth century by a prior from the charterhouse. This small, plain building became a place of pilgrimage after the reformation; from the chapel, the view into the Vale of Mowbray below is excellent.

Walkers may stroll the entire ridge of the Hambleton Hills using the Cleveland Way. Although there are fine, panoramic views for much of the distance, the walker, for once, might see less of the countryside than the driver or cycler who uses the back roads along the hillside to head south. A journey leaving the A19 three miles south of Mount Grace and beginning at Over Silton has much to commend it.

After passing through Over Silton and glancing towards its church, St Mary, turn right at the T-junction for Nether Silton; here the church is nineteenth century but the hall sixteenth century, though the castellated tower dates from 1838.

A left at the junction then a left, right and left will eventually bring the traveller to Cowesby, where the church of 1846 is by Anthony Salvin, a pupil of John Nash who specialised in country houses. Indeed, the original Cowesby Hall was also built by Salvin;

this was in 1832, but we are too late to see it, as the new model arrived in 1949.

Turn right out of Cowesby, and two miles on is Kirby Knowle; here, turn left for Felixkirk and the A170 at Sutton under Whitestonecliffe. Head east for the magnificent climb of Sutton Bank, a rise of 500 feet in half a mile.

The gradient here is as steep as one in four, but the reward is the endless, seamless view across the vale to the Pennines and perhaps the whole of England. A well-walked track leads south from the brow, past the gliding club airstrip and along the top of the escarpment. At Roulston Scar, where the path bends east, the view west takes in the conical outlier Hood Hill, with its overgrown Iron Age earthworks.

Continue a little further and the village of Kilburn will be only a mile away, directly below to the south; almost under your feet will be the White Horse, a gargantuan steed cut from the turf and revealed by the clay beneath (with a little help from lime and chalk dressings). Paradoxically it is so big, at two acres, that when close its impact is lessened by its huge size. The animal is best viewed from below, and can be seen even at a distance of thirty miles. There is a seat by its tail, and it is somehow disconcerting to discover that its eye is a great grass hummock. Originally the idea of Thomas Taylor of Kilburn, it was carved from the hillside in 1857. Thirty people took two months to excavate the horse, which measures 314 feet in length and 228 feet in height.

If Taylor's intention was to create a symbol of the Hambleton Hills, one similar to the chalk figures of the southern downs, he succeeded. Horse-racing began in the

Hambleton area in the late sixteenth century, the track being about a mile north of Sutton Bank. It was a popular venue until its best race was transferred to York in 1755, after which it declined and the final meeting was held in 1811, although training still takes place on the turf gallops. Maybe the White Horse was the dream horse of Thomas Taylor, forever standing at the winning post of life on the hills above his home.

LAST TRAIN TO THE QUEEN OF THE NORTH

Scarborough and the Vale of Pickering

T HE ATTRACTION of the view from the jutting limestone headland of Castle Hill in Scarborough has remained constant since Bronze Age settlers made their home on its easternmost side. Sands to north and south, the moors to the north-west, and inland that huge basin, the Vale of Pickering, cut off from the sea by Scarborough's own hilly site.

A Roman signal station stood on Castle Hill in the late fourth century, but the real foundation date of the town was around 966, when it was home to a Danish community. This, however, remained only until Scarborough was overrun by the Norse invasion of 1066.

Building of the castle on the headland was begun a little before 1135 by William le Gros, later created Earl of Yorkshire after his part in the victory over the Scots at the Battle of the Standard, which was fought out near Northallerton in 1138. Scarborough Castle became the earl's main stronghold, but the campaign of Henry II to reduce baronial power

led to its eventual surrender. The king retained the castle and added the splendid keep between 1158 and 1168. Although severely damaged during and after the Civil War, the ruins of the keep still dominate the headland.

Scarborough itself developed on the neck of land immediately inland from the castle; this Old Borough was extended into the New Borough, slightly to the west, in the thirteenth century. The town relied for its prosperity on the shipping trade, and would in all probability have remained a port to this day but for one Mrs Farrer, who in 1626 discovered a mineral spring on the south shore. Within forty years its medicinal properties had become widely known and Scarborough had acquired the status of a spa town. By the early eighteenth century, visitors were arriving from outside Yorkshire to take the waters, and sea bathing was first noted in Scarborough around 1730. Thus was born the English seaside resort.

Initially, Scarborough was deemed physically unattractive to visitors because of its steep cliffs, but by 1725 it at least provided rooms

The South Bay, Scarborough, in the early twentieth century. Bass Brewery excursions visited the resort eight times between 1881 and the final brewery trip in 1914.

for public assembly. The townspeople were slow to see the need for public walks and entertainment buildings, and in the league of northern spa towns Scarborough was overtaken by Harrogate during the nineteenth century. Salvation appeared in the unlikely form of a trickle of working class visitors, which grew to a deluge after the arrival of the railway in 1845. Weekends in Scarborough were never to be the same again.

There was much expansion of resort activities in the town during the middle of the nineteenth century, but a decline around the turn of the century, when newer and perhaps more modern resorts became popular. Between 1881 and 1911 Scarborough sank from sixth to thirteenth largest of the English and Welsh resorts. Seaside pleasure buildings underwent a national construction boom during 1870-1910, and the early establishment of Scarborough as a resort-cum-spa, followed by the late nineteenth century period of slow growth, explains the lack of these substantial pleasure buildings in the town.

Scarborough's sheer size, with twin beaches and lengthy promenades, did mean that it could accommodate the largest of day trips, even the monstrous annual day excursion from the Bass Brewery at Burton-upon-Trent. From 1889 onwards, up to fifteen trains would leave Burton for Blackpool, New Brighton, Great Yarmouth or Scarborough, depositing 10,000 employees and their families beside the sea. It was a long day out; on the 24th July 1914, the last train of what was to be the very last excursion left Burton at 6.00am, arriving

A holiday snap with early beach chalets in the background; probably the North Bay at Scarborough between the wars.

at Scarborough four hours later. The party were allowed almost thirteen hours of fun and games before catching the 10.55pm home, arriving at Burton just after three in the morning.

Had any Bass trippers visited the castle, they would have been charged two pence for admission and seen the view much as it is today; indeed, the town's modern attractions differ only a little from those described in the official Bass excursion handbook to the 'Queen of Watering Places' or the 'Queen of the North'.

From the castle, then, for a quick exploration of the town, first head west across the headland along Castle Road to the parish church of St Mary. Part of the fabric of the church dates from the late twelfth century, but it was greatly expanded around 1450. The crossing tower fell in 1659 and was rebuilt ten years later, and additional restoration took place in 1848 and 1950. The churchyard offers a fine view over the town, and in its eastern extension is the grave of Anne Brontë.

A steep descent via the steps below St Mary's, which lead to Church Stairs Street then St Mary's Street, brings the walker to the waterside at the West Pier. The harbour is enclosed by the West Pier, which was built in 1817, and the East Pier, much strengthened around 1790-1812. Harbour and outer harbour are divided by Vincent's Pier, completed by 1752, with its lighthouse dating from 1800. The lighthouse was damaged by a German shell during the First World War and was rebuilt in 1931.

Foreshore Road leads along by the South Sands; in the distance, just above the beach, stands the Spa Building. It was designed by London theatre architects Thomas Verity and

The Spa Building, standing above the South Sands at Scarborough, was erected in 1877-80 and redeveloped as an entertainments and conference centre in 1979-85.

G H Hunt to replace Sir Joseph Paxton's 1857 Grand Hall, which was burnt out in 1876. The new Spa, erected in 1877-80, combined the functions of theatre, hall and baths, the latter complete with colourful tiling, but although appearing romantic when seen at a distance, the building is now rather a shadow of its original self.

Press on past the beckoning arcades to the cliff lift, which will trundle you up to the edifice which has come to symbolise the English seaside resort just as Leeds Town Hall embodies the whole of Victorian municipal culture. It is fitting, then, that the architect of the Grand Hotel should also have

designed the Leeds trademark. Cuthbert Brodrick followed his Leeds Town Hall of 1853-8 by producing the huge Grand Hotel for the Scarborough Cliff Hotel Company in 1863-7. The company ran out of funds before building was half-finished, and the prospective white elephant was auctioned off cheaply to a Leeds businessman, who had the nerve to complete the hotel to its original plan.

The thirteen storeys of this statuesque, four-domed leviathan contain 365 rooms and rise to 160 feet above the sea. Building materials were red and yellow brick, and the style perhaps the vaguest of Second Empire, but mere stylistic considerations seem inconsequential in the face of such a crushing piece of architecture. Despite a frequently hazardous financial situation, the hotel has survived and still performs its original function, although

The silhouetted Cliff Bridge, Scarborough. It was built by the Cliff Bridge Company in 1826-7 at a cost of just over £9,000, and it combines local stone with ironwork from Bradford. The domes of Cuthbert Brodrick's Grand Hotel are to the left, and in the distance is the castle.

the decorative interior has been toned down and the lofty lounge is gloomy rather than glorious.

The Valley south of the hotel may be crossed via Cliff Bridge, built in 1826-7 to connect town with spa. Its four cast iron arches span a total width of 414 feet, and the pedestrian bridge allows a fine view of the north slope of the Valley. Here stands the elegant purpose-built Rotunda Museum, a Classical cylinder designed in 1828-9 by architect Richard Hey Sharp while he was still working on the Greek Revival-style Yorkshire Museum at York. Sharp, with his partner and younger brother Samuel — who had assisted with the Rotunda design — went on to plan the further development of the Valley, including the Crescent, just west of the Rotunda. The presence of the high-living Yorkshire landowner Lord Londesborough at Londesborough Lodge, just below the Crescent, attracted society and money to the town, particularly during the third quarter of the nineteenth century.

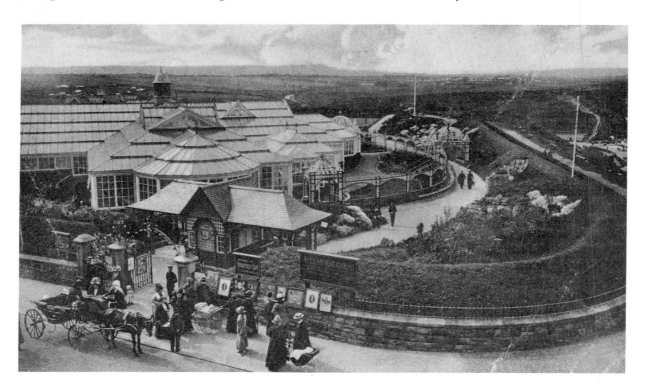

An early view of the Floral Hall, Scarborough, a winter garden-style theatre built in 1911 close to the North Sands.

Almost below Cliff Bridge is the site of the lamented Aquarium, an exotic Indo-Moorish entertainment centre opened in 1877 and designed by Eugenius Birch, builder of piers, railways, harbours and pier pavilions in Britain and abroad.

The wildly extravagant Aquarium was not at first a success, but when converted to the People's Palace in 1886 by offering cheap all-day entertainment, visitors poured in. The fortunes of the Aquarium slowly declined after the First World War, and the site was cleared in 1968 to make way for an unspeakably seedy underground car park. Thus came the end of one of England's best seaside buildings.

The tale of woe concerning pleasure buildings continues with the recent destruction of the glasshouse-style Floral Hall Theatre (1911), not far from the North Sands in Alexandra Gardens, to be replaced by a bowls centre. Neighbouring Peasholm Park, an Edwardian essay in Japanese style successfully applied to a Yorkshire municipal park (the thirty foot pagoda was added in 1929), is fortunately still with us.

It is tempting to carry on across Cliff Bridge to the delights of the South Cliff, but a trip back to the railway station (head west from the Grand Hotel) is worthwhile. Its memorable if overbearing Baroque clock-tower was an addition of 1884 to the original 1845 Classical design by G T Andrews for the York and North Midland Railway.

Across the road is the Odeon, a 1936 job by Cecil Clavering from the Odeon architect Harry Weedon's practice in Birmingham. The typical cream and black ceramic façade is laced with red, while the original interior has

The parish church of St Mary, Scarborough, was damaged during the Civil War, causing the crossing tower to collapse fourteen years later in 1659; rebuilding took place within ten years. The tower clock was installed in 1856.

recently been the subject of controversial alterations, changing its function from cinema to theatre. The elegant Odeon Obelisk — the cinema chain's trademark — which originally stood at the centre of the nearby road junction,

The clock tower of Scarborough railway station, an 1884 addition to the original structure. The four clock faces were lit by gas until 1970.

Sunday in Scarborough earlier this century: time for church parade, along the Esplanade. In the distance, to the right, is the Grand Hotel.

has recently been moved a little to the west, and now stands between Odeon and station.

Despite the existence of the elegant terrace of the Esplanade on the South Cliff, developed from the 1840s, the premier building south of

the valley is a church, St Martin-on-the-Hill in Albion Road. St Martin stands across Valley Bridge from the railway station, or inland from the Esplanade at its north end; nearing the church, look out for the jolly frieze of colourful sculpted heads on the terrace to the south.

St Martin contains a wonderful display of Pre-Raphaelite decorative work dating from 1861-73, all financed by a Scarborough lady,

The Crown Hotel on the Esplanade, South Cliff, Scarborough, around 1890. The hotel, which opened about 1844, was part of the earliest developments on the Esplanade.

Mary Craven. The church was built in 1861-3 and designed by G F Bodley, who brought in Morris, Marshall, Faulkner & Co to work on the interior. It is a gem: William Morris, Philip Webb, Burne-Jones, Rossetti and others combined to produce the stained glass, and there is painted decoration on ceilings and pulpit — in fact colour and delight all around. See this, even if you see nothing else in Scarborough.

Heading south out of Scarborough along Filey Road (A167), a mile or so from Valley Bridge we come across one last viewpoint in this hilly town. The war memorial obelisk on Oliver's Mount may be reached from the main road via Mountside and an anticlockwise climb. There are great views of sea and shore, and the wooded hill provides a fine last glimpse of the coast for those about to explore the vale to the west.

An early twentieth century view of Pickering market place.

The River Derwent rises on Fylingdales Moor and flows south to a point just south-west of Scarborough, thence through the Vale of Pickering. Its course may be intercepted before it leaves the moors at Hackness, six miles from Scarborough (take the A171 north and turn off at Scalby).

Here, steep dales lead up into the moors to north and west, while the picturesque village was rebuilt by Lord Derwent of Hackness Hall in the nineteenth century. The hall was built in 1797 by Peter Atkinson the elder, assistant to John Carr, and with its stables and

other ancilliary buildings makes a fine Georgian estate complex.

The road and assorted footpaths lead south to the A170, the main road running across the vale at the foot of the moors, passing through the natural woodland of Forge Valley on the way.

Just over a mile south of Hackness the road crosses the Sea Cut, the original course of the Derwent prior to the Ice Age, when its eastward route to the sea was blocked by glacial boulder clay. The Forge Valley gorge was scoured out by meltwater leaving the

Vale of Pickering prone to flooding, and the Sea Cut was dug in 1800-4 to rectify this by allowing the flow of the Derwent to be controlled by weirs.

Ayton, with its ruined but pretty fourteenth century pele tower (a fortified tower house), marks the return to the busy main road. Press on west through Wykeham, with its set of William Butterfield buildings comprising church (1853), school and vicarage; the estate to the south of the road belongs to Wykeham Abbey, built in 1904 by Banbury architect N R Mills and named after the twelfth century nunnery which stood on the site of the church.

Ebberston, with its delightful miniature hall, lies five miles further west. Ebberston Hall was built in 1718 by Colen Campbell, doyen of the Palladian movement, but the style is more that of a rustic garden folly. The tiny three-bay hall rises only a single storey above a concealed basement. The intention was to build further pavilions, but only the water garden was ever laid out, with a cascade and a 1,200 foot canal. The gardens have now disappeared, leaving the jolly little lodge all alone.

The attractive village of Thornton Dale, with its almshouses, stream and bridges, lies on the westward route to the hilly market town of Pickering, where the castle gives good views all around. It dates generally from the twelfth to early fourteenth centuries; the well-preserved shell keep, set upon its artificial hill or motte above Pickering Beck, was built about 1220-30.

The real star of Pickering is the church of St Peter and St Paul, basically Norman but with many later alterations. The fabric of the church is of less import than the set of mid-fifteenth century wall paintings, which — although heavily restored in 1880 — at least give the twentieth century visitor a chance to see how the interior of a medieval church actually looked. The largely black and red paintings run throughout the nave and inventively show scenes from the lives of the saints.

The Catholic church of St Joseph stands west of the bridge, on Potter Hill. The towered Tudoresque building was designed in 1907-11 by Leonard Stokes, the London-based architect known for his work throughout the country on Catholic churches and schools between the 1880s and the First World War, as well as his series of telephone exchanges built for the National Telephone Company in 1898-1908. The tall font at St Joseph is by Eric Gill, who decorated its octagonal bowl with figures and leaves in his usual spare, unmistakable style.

Heading west of Pickering along the A170, a side road leads to Sinnington, with its Norman church; back on the main road, the traveller should then turn north (soon after Kirkbymoorside) into Kirkdale, the valley of Hodge Beck, to come upon the totally unexpected: a Saxon church, St Gregory's Minster, at Kirkdale. It nestles in a secluded, wooded site beside the beck, an idyllic situation which perhaps has changed little since late Saxon times, when the original church was built. In 1060 — as recorded by the sundial above the south doorway — the church was rebuilt, and the chancel was added in 1881. These and other alterations have given the structure a strange asymmetry, but the nave remains massively Saxon.

West again, five miles on to the noble market town of Helmsley. Before the end of the

Raising the maypole at Sinnington, near Pickering, in 1929.

eleventh century, Helmsley was a hamlet of little importance, but around that time the manor passed into the hands of the l'Espec family. Walter l'Espec, a northern baron who helped to defeat the Scots at the Battle of the Standard, was Lord of Helmsley during 1120-54, and selected the hamlet as the site for his castle. This proved the key to future growth, and by the late twelfth century the expanding village had become prosperous; by the end of the medieval period it was an important market centre, with farming and weaving as its main sources of income.

The fortunes of the town were at their highest during the eighteenth century. Weaving of wool, then locally-grown flax for linen, had ensured prosperity, but the early nineteenth century saw stiff competition from the West Riding textile industry, and by 1834 only two working looms remained in Helmsley. The town reverted to agricultural and estate interests; part of the Feversham estate, Duncombe Park, lies immediately south-west of Helmsley. This avoidance of nineteenth and twentieth century industrial development has turned out well for Helmsley, now a strong tourist centre which has lost none of its original charm.

The gaunt and lofty remains of Helmsley Castle stand on a rocky ridge above the River Rye, which flows just to the south of the town. The keep and parts of the curtain wall date from the end of the twelfth century, while the west range was rebuilt at some point between

1563 and 1587; the interior of the west range shows fine wood-panelling.

For a sight of town, castle and vale, walk a little way along the footpath which ascends the hill to the west from close by the castle car park; this is the start of the Cleveland Way, which within minutes rewards the walker with a panoramic view to the east. As the path rises it also reveals the Ionic temple lurking in the grounds of Duncombe Park to the south; the town gate of the park is just beyond the southern end of the market place.

A complex and lengthy history of inheritance, marriage and finally debt lies behind the purchase of the Helmsley and Rievaulx estates in 1687 by wealthy banker Sir Charles Duncombe, who later became Lord Mayor of London. Duncombe appears to have taken little interest in his Yorkshire acquisition, and after his death in 1711 the lands passed to his brother-in-law, Thomas Brown, who promptly changed his name to Duncombe. He quickly began to build a substantial house at Helmsley. The heavily Baroque mansion was completed in 1713 and also named after Sir Charles; it was designed by Yorkshire gentleman architect William Wakefield, who was probably advised by Sir John Vanbrugh.

The house is complemented by a delightful curving half-mile terrace overlooking the Rye; this was laid out soon after 1713 and equipped with Classical temples at either end. To the north is the wholly open Ionic temple, built around 1718 by Vanbrugh, while the circular Tuscan temple to the south was added slightly later. This early combination of Classical formalism with a natural setting may be due to landscape gardener Charles Bridgeman, best known for his work at Stowe. Thomas

Duncombe III, who inherited the estate in 1746, built a similar terrace, complete with Classical temples, at Rievaulx around 1751-61, but there the style was altogether more Picturesque.

Thomas Duncombe III died in 1799 and his property eventually passed to his nephew, created Lord Feversham in 1826. Feversham's grandson commissioned Charles Barry to extend the house in 1843-6, but fires in 1879 and 1894 resulted in great destruction, and apart from the façade the house of today is largely a rebuilding (to the original Wakefield design) of 1895. House and grounds remain, however, crucial to the history of English landscape gardening.

The aimiable centre of Helmsley, the market place, is ornamented by a conclusively Gothic monument to the second Lord Feversham, who died in 1867; his statue is overwhelmed by a frilly canopy designed by Sir George Gilbert Scott in 1869-71, even as he worked on the Albert Memorial in London's Hyde Park.

The church of All Saints lies just to the north-west of the market square. It was established in the eleventh century but the oldest part of the current structure, the south doorway and chancel arches, dates from a twelfth century reconstruction. A tower and north aisle were added in the following century, but the church as we see it today largely results from rebuilding in 1849 and 1866-9. The exterior is unremarkable but the interior is a blaze of colour, an extravagant memorial to the taste of Vicar Charles Norris Gray, who arrived at Helmsley in 1870.

Gray must have come as an intense culture shock to the people of the small rural town. He was at war with dissent, a social reformer forever writing and researching on a wide range of subjects, a hard-working trainer of clergy, and a man who began every day with a cold bath taken at six in the morning. As his services started to emphasise the gulf between the traditional church and dissenters, he began to add colour to the church itself by introducing stained glass and wall painting. Murals adorn the north aisle, where the ceiling painting of 1909 is by Temple Moore, and in the Columba Chapel (south transept) a tremendous dragon is impaled by a lance. Gray's energies extended to the building of churches in several local hamlets; he died, not surprisingly of overwork, in 1913.

One of Vicar Gray's churches stands at Sproxton, two miles south of Helmsley. Take the main A170, which bends west at the Nelson Arch on the edge of Duncombe Park. This triumphal gateway, though typical of the high-status entrance buildings to be found on many eighteenth century English estates, was built in 1806 to commemorate the 1805 Battle of Trafalgar.

Almost opposite the archway, the B1257 leads off towards Sproxton and eventually Malton. The tiny church of St Chad at Sproxton is actually an Elizabethan chapel which was moved from a nearby hall in 1879 at the behest of Lord Feversham and Vicar Gray. Architects for its rebuilding were George Gilbert Scott junior and his assistant Temple Lushington Moore; the latter worked on many Yorkshire churches. The unusual interior of St Chad has interesting wood carvings and stained glass.

Two miles further in the direction of Malton at Oswaldkirk Bank Top, a by-road takes the traveller west towards Byland Abbey, passing the fine collection of college buildings at Ampleforth. The Catholic public school of Ampleforth College was founded in 1802 by Benedictine monks, and most of the school's eclectic collection of buildings — along with a fine view over the valley of the Holbeck to the Howardian Hills — may be seen from the road. The elegant abbey church was built between 1922 and 1961; the cool Gothic structure was designed by Sir Giles Gilbert Scott, pupil of Temple Moore and architect of Liverpool's Anglican Cathedral. North of the road is the bow-windowed St Wilfrid's and St Edward's Houses (1934), trenchant thirties architecture in a sun trap on the hillside.

Two miles south of Oswaldkirk on the B1363 is Gilling Castle, standing above the village of Gilling East. The house, a short essay in architectural history but mainly a combination of Elizabethan and eighteenth century work, occupies three sides of a quadrangle and is partly built on fourteenth century foundations. The great chamber, though, dates from around 1575-85 and has a fine chimneypiece and excellent wall-panelling.

If deviations to Ampleforth and Gilling do not appeal, carry on along the Malton road through Stonegrave, turning north a mile past the village for Nunnington, where Nunnington Hall lies on the banks of the Rye. On this tranquil site was first a Saxon homestead, but the earliest part of the present house dates from the mid-sixteenth century, and most of the homely, tall-chimneyed mansion is seventeenth century work. This is due to Richard Graham, first Viscount Preston and Master of the Wardrobe to James II, who inherited the estate in 1685. The elegant south front faces a charming walled garden, a symmetrical survivor of later Picturesque trends in landscaping. Perhaps the new fashion passed by this remote and watery outpost.

Head back to the Malton road, down the steep ridge of Caulkley's Bank, and press on a mile or so for Hovingham, where the Worsley Arms stands by the village green. This Georgian pub is named after the owners of Hovingham Park, which extends to the west of the village centre.

The approach to Hovingham Hall is unusual; a tall, tunnel vaulted archway leads straight into the riding school and thence the Palladian house. Both were designed in the 1750s by Thomas Worsley, later Surveyor of the Office of Works, whose great interests in life were horses and architecture. His new home was a happy combination of these powerful forces. The church of All Saints is close by the hall, and harbours several monuments to the Worsleys as well as its great treasure, a Saxon slab carved with figures, which acts as a reredos.

Once upon a time a John Carr house, dating from around 1780, stood at Wiganthorpe Park, three miles south of Hovingham in the Howardian Hills, but it was demolished in 1955.

However, the remains of the mansion at Slingsby, two miles east along the B1257, do still exist. Slingsby Castle was built around the 1640s for Sir Charles Cavendish, grandson of Bess of Hardwick, by John Smythson. Cavendish's father intended to build at Slingsby about 1599, and commissioned Robert Smythson, father of John and the leading architect of his era in the North, to produce a plan. Robert Smythson's design incorporated the moat of ancient Slingsby Castle; the new castle would have risen from the water in a surge of turrets and towers, but was never built. The substantial ruins of John Smythson's castle suggest a handsome, many-windowed building, but not quite the fairy-tale castle of his father's imagination.

Onwards to Malton, through Barton-le-Street and its Norman cum neo-Norman church of St Michael, where twelfth century carving and its upstart 1871 imitation make a happy mix.

Malton, on the west bank of the Derwent, originated a mile upstream at the agricultural village of Old Malton. The planned borough of New Malton grew into a thriving market town and became a centre for the brewing industry.

The church of St Mary at Old Malton is the sole remaining part of a Gilbertine priory founded on the site around 1147. The Gilbertines were England's only home-grown monastic order, founded in 1131 by one Gilbert, a parish priest at Sempringham in Lincolnshire. His attempt to persuade the Cistercians to take over the growing order in 1147 was rebuffed, and the Gilbertines continued with their unique regulations, which included a powerful role for nuns in mixed monasteries (although there were never any nuns at Old Malton, which was solely for men). They gained a high reputation for their work amongst the rural poor. The west front of St Mary is monumental, with the late Norman doorway topped by a large Perpendicular window, and beside it the single surviving tower.

Back in Malton, the new town has an abundance of interesting alleyways, shop-

St Gregory's Minster at Kirkdale, a Saxon church in a beautiful setting.

The Ionic temple, built around 1718 by Vanbrugh, and the Father Time sundial on the terrace at Duncombe Park, near Helmsley.

The gaunt ruins of Slingsby Castle, built around the 1640s by John Smythson for Sir Charles Cavendish.

fronts and changes of level, and is focussed on Market Place, with its eighteenth century town hall (now a museum) and the much-restored Norman church of St Michael. St Leonard on Church Hill (take the lane leading off the main east-west road by the White Swan) contains an iron monument to local ironfounder Arthur Gibson, who died in 1837. He designed his own memorial, which shows him at prayer and enjoying a drink.

The most enjoyable means of leaving Malton is surely the train south, which hugs the Derwent as it wriggles between the Howardian Hills and the Wolds, before heading off to York. There are fine views of Kirkham Priory and Howsham Hall, across the border in the East Riding.

Once there was a station at Huttons Ambo, three miles out of Malton, where an elegant, green suspension bridge crosses the river; another station served one of the greatest palaces in the country, for now we are nearing Castle Howard. But today these stations are no more, and the architectural traveller must approach Castle Howard more prosaically by road — via the A64 — or even on foot. Although the grand plan unfolds as its maker intended for those who follow the carriage route, several footpaths cross the estate for those seeking a less-regimented view of the ultimate garden.

The story of Castle Howard begins in the summer of 1698, when Charles Howard, third Earl of Carlisle, visited the tiny village of Henderskelfe, about five miles west of Malton and perched in the hills above the Vale of Pickering. The earl, whose family home was in rustic Cumberland, had latterly become attracted to fashionable London life and was

The great dome and south front of Castle Howard, built in 1701-12 by Vanbrugh and Hawksmoor for the third Earl of Carlisle.

beginning to take an interest in artistic matters, probably as a result of his three year Grand Tour. Henderskelfe and the remains of its castle — it had been burnt down in 1693 — was the property of his grandparents, but he took out a lease on the estate and retired to London to consider the development of his new plaything.

The massive form of the Carrmire Gate, built in 1728 by Hawksmoor, guards the southern approach to Castle Howard.

The time was right for architectural statements; the accession of William and Mary to the throne a few years previously in 1689 had brought with it a new interest in building, and Howard was a politically ambitious man who could hope to impress in high places through overseeing the construction of a great house, which would also emphasise the nobility of his ancestry. As to the design of the house, the earl first consulted gentleman-architect and country-house specialist William Talman, but dispensed with his services in summer 1699 and asked a friend, John Vanbrugh — then known only as a playwright — to take on the task. He set to with enthusiasm.

The south — or garden — front of Castle Howard, with the mid-nineteenth century Triton Fountain in the foreground. The sculptor of the central figure, Atlas bearing a globe, was John Thomas, a favourite of Prince Albert.

By late 1700 a model of Castle Howard was being shown around London, and doubtless much discussed, but it was spring 1701 before the foundations were begun. Vanbrugh hired Nicholas Hawksmoor, then clerk of works to Sir Christopher Wren, to supervise construction on a daily basis. In summer 1709 the exterior was more or less complete, but furnishing and decorating the interior took until around the end of 1712.

By this time the earl had become heavily involved with his castle; his political ambitions had been frustrated, and now all his energy and most of his money (from his estates and

The Temple of the Four Winds at Castle Howard was designed by Vanbrugh in 1723-4, but not completed until 1737; the mausoleum stands in the distance.

his frequently successful forays to the gambling tables) were taken up with house and park. Until his death in 1738, at the age of sixty-nine, the earl concentrated upon adding majestic architectural ornaments to his already palatial estate.

Passing the column erected in 1869-70 in memory of the seventh earl, the southern approach to Castle Howard begins with a descent towards the Carrmire Gate, built in 1728 by Hawksmoor. It is a crushing gateway decked out with pyramids and set into a neo-medieval wall with menacing corner bastions.

Up the hill to the Pyramid Lodge, this time by Vanbrugh himself and designed in 1719; it is a hulking pyramid atop an arch, and allows the intrepid visitor entry through a castellated wall with another glorious array of bastions,

The Pyramid Lodge, built in 1719, and the distant obelisk, erected in 1714, are but two of the architectural highlights on the southern approach to Castle Howard.

The mausoleum is the final resting place of the third Earl of Carlisle, creator of its sublime surroundings. He died in 1738, although Hawksmoor's massive temple was not complete until 1745.

built in 1719-23. Ahead is Vanbrugh's obelisk of 1714, where a right turn leads at last to Castle Howard.

The north front of the house, a huge and heady Baroque pile dominated by its dome, looks towards the North York Moors. Inside is the monumental great hall, fit for a royal palace and lit by the dome, which was originally decorated with paintings by Pellegrini; dome and paintings were destroyed in the disastrous fire of 1940, but rebuilding has not lessened the grandeur of the concept.

The Broad Walk runs across the south façade, and leads east to the Terrace Walk, which curves away around Ray Wood towards the Temple of the Four Winds. This miniature Italian villa was designed by Vanbrugh in 1723-4, but the architect had been dead over ten years before the completion of the interior around 1737.

The park holds yet more theatrical effects: a pyramid, a Roman bridge, and, finally, a mausoleum.

This was a display of wealth on a vast scale, a response to the Grand Tour, and an assertion of indifference to political power. The earl's castle had become his home. His resting place was to be Hawksmoor's mausoleum, planned from the early 1720s but not ready to receive the earl until 1745. The mausoleum is a massive domed cylinder with an outer ring of Tuscan columns. Its phenomenal form adds the finishing touch to the Castle Howard landscape of dreams, transformed by the earl from windswept hill to another country.

Where family and politics failed the earl, his castle sustained him. He reached beyond the mundane to create a heavenly landscape, peopled with buildings of his imagination; his fulfilment was to remain there forever.

MEANDERING THROUGH THE VALE

The Vale of York

FOUR RUINED and craggy towers silhouetted against the sky mark the village of Sheriff Hutton, marooned on the very edge of the Howardian Hills. York is only ten miles to the south but the village is relatively remote, lying just above the valley of the River Foss (which joins the Ouse at York), and between the Scarborough and Helmsley roads.

The towers of Sheriff Hutton castle once rose to four or even five storeys and were connected to form a courtyard. Building began soon after 1382, although an earlier version erected by the Sheriff of Yorkshire (from whom the village took its name) stood south of the church. The castle played its part in the Wars of the Roses, at one time belonging to Richard III, but faced dereliction by the middle of the seventeenth century. A footpath leads round the castle from Castle Farm, just off daffodil-lined Main Street.

Main Street descends slowly eastward through the village to the church of St Helen and the Holy Cross, where Edward, Prince of Wales and son of Richard III, lies buried. He

One of Sheriff Hutton Castle's four ruined towers.

The church of St Helen and the Holy Cross, Sheriff Hutton, is the burial place of Edward, Prince of Wales, who died in 1484. His grandfather, Richard, Earl of Warwick, was the owner of Sheriff Hutton Castle.

died in 1484 at Middleham Castle, a year before his father was slain at the Battle of Bosworth Field, which ended the Yorkist era. Edward only reached eleven years of age and his alabaster monument, a boyish effigy, stands in the north-east chapel.

The church itself is built of a pleasing mix of limestone and sandstone, and dates from Norman times, although additions and rebuildings took place in the thirteenth and fourteenth centuries. The two chapels were added in the late fifteenth century. There are fine views from the churchyard.

South-east of the village is Sheriff Hutton Hall, built by Sir Arthur Ingram in 1619-24, just before his massive rebuilding of Temple Newsam House near Leeds. The house was designed in the style of Robert Smythson, and built (like Temple Newsam) in brick, but its façade dates from 1732 alterations. Further east of Sheriff Hutton, through Thornton-le-Clay, is the village of Foston, where the Norman doorway of All Saints Church displays a collection of scenes ranging from the Last Supper to wrestlers and nameless beasts.

The East Riding is a mere four miles from Foston, across the A64 at Barton Hill and down to the Derwent, which forms the border, at Howsham Bridge. Here a footpath runs north along the riverside, in a mile or so allowing the walker a view of stunning Howsham Hall on the far bank, built around 1619 and also in the Smythson style.

The road south from Howsham bridge rises well above the river to pass through Bossall, with its moated, seventeenth century hall; the church of St Botolph has a peculiar square font bowl, perhaps dating from the twelfth century.

Sheriff Hutton lies only two miles from the River Foss, whose banks may be walked upstream or down. The southward journey takes the walker through the suburb of New Earswick, on the northern fringe of the city of York.

Although its original plan has become somewhat submerged by later development, the core of New Earswick is one of England's most successful industrial model villages, built from 1902-3 for Joseph Rowntree and his son Seebohm, the Quakers and chocolate manufacturers.

The housing — bright pantiled terraces — was designed by Raymond Unwin and Barry Parker, leading theorists and practitioners of the Arts and Crafts style of architecture and planning. Gardens and ample common ground were provided, and an institute, later named the Folk Hall, was added in 1908 to supply the communal focal-point normally associated with a church. The factory was only a bicycle ride away, but did not dominate the village, which was not intended solely for Rowntree workers. Even today New Earswick retains a mellow and relaxed air.

Three miles west of New Earswick, the River Ouse interrupts the progress of the traveller across the Vale of York, and defines the edge of the West Riding. The busy A19 follows the river roughly north-west, reaching Skelton about four miles out from the city.

Here stands the little church of St Giles, erected around 1247 and stylistically in the same vein as York Minster; indeed, its building was financed by the treasurer of the Minster. The ornate detailing is perhaps partly original, partly due to a restoration of 1814-18 by Henry Graham, son of a York rector. Skelton

New Earswick, near York, photographed from the air around 1916. The village, begun in 1902, originated with Joseph Rowntree's belief that it was possible to provide decent housing for workers on low incomes.

Employees of the Rowntree chocolate factory at York on a cricket outing to the pretty village of Thornton Dale, near Pickering, in 1936.

The Folk Hall, built in 1908, was the communal centre of the Rowntree model village New Earswick.

The newly-opened extension to New Earswick's Folk Hall, 1935. The community centre was modernised in 1968.

comprised Graham's entire career as an architect; he was only nineteen when the work began, and soon after its completion he left for Italy, where he met his death in 1819. His monument at Skelton refers to the 'corrupting air of foreign lands'.

Turn off the A19 two miles further north near Shipton to find Beningbrough Hall, beautifully situated in parkland — mainly water-meadows — on the east bank of the Ouse. The Beningbrough estate was granted by Henry VIII to John Banister in 1544, but later passed to the family of his son-in-law, the Bourchiers; Sir Ralph Bourchier built on the estate in the late sixteenth century, but John Bourchier pulled down this house and erected the present hall, which was completed by 1716.

The fine eleven-bay house, built in red brick with stone dressings, was probably designed by a combination of William Thornton of York, architect and carpenter, and gentleman-architect Thomas Archer, who added the Italian Baroque elements. Altogether it is one of the best surviving examples of the English Baroque house. The interior is dominated by passages running north-south and east-west, and the most impressive room is the double-height great hall, which is entered immediately from the north front and is adorned with pilasters and plasterwork.

A by-road leads west from Newton-on-Ouse, just north of Beningbrough, following the course of the river to Aldwark, where a delightful bridge and an idiosyncratic church may be found. St Stephen, designed in 1846-53 by E B Lamb, has a polychromatic exterior and a high roof with complex timbering. This is typical of Lamb's style, which was always a picturesque version of Gothic relatively unaffected by the current ecclesiastically-correct fashions.

Three miles north-east is Alne, where the Norman church of St Mary boasts a highly-decorative south doorway, alive with signs of the zodiac and strange animals.

Head east from the village and cross the A19 to find Sutton-on-the Forest and Sutton Park, built between 1750 and 1764 in the style of James Paine, with a pediment covering all five bays of the main block; there are two linked pavilions. With the brick façade of the house as a backdrop, the elegant gardens form a pleasant interlude in a journey through the vale.

Leaving Sutton behind, travel north on the B1363 and look for the pretty village of Crayke to the north-west, occupying a small hill separated from the nearby Howardian Hills by the upper Foss Valley. (To reach the village, take the Easingwold road at Stillington, then turn north after a couple of miles.) The church of St Cuthbert dates from the Perpendicular period, between the early fourteenth and early sixteenth centuries, and has good Jacobean pews, but the major landmark of Crayke is the castle. It was built on the site of a Norman castle and is actually two separate fifteenth century buildings, the main one being a tower house.

Five miles of by-road lie between Crayke and Newburgh Priory, on the northern edge of the Howardian Hills. The road leaves Crayke from close by church and castle, running north through Oulston and over the hills, which face the Hambleton Hills to the north across Gilling Gap (in which rivers appear to flow in all directions).

The priory originated around 1150 as an Augustinian foundation. It was dissolved in 1529 and little of the monastic buildings remain. The long, low house known as Newburgh Priory dates from the sixteenth to eighteenth centuries; inside, the hall has a tremendous alabaster and marble overmantel, with assorted figures and columns.

Less than a mile up the road from Newburgh is the still-quiet village of Coxwold. The striking octagonal tower of fifteenth century St Michael's Church stands out above the wide grass verges and demure cottages.

Laurence Sterne came to live in Coxwold soon after publishing the first part of *The Life and Opinions of Tristram Shandy*, which has come to be seen as a unique and innovatory work, a precursor of twentieth century stream-of-conciousness writing.

Sterne made his home at a farmhouse on the western edge of the village, which he named Shandy Hall. Prior to his excursion into print, Sterne had been just another obscure country clergyman, albeit the grandson of an Archbishop of York and a man with a taste for good living. He was Vicar of Coxwold until his death in 1768.

Only a couple of miles north-east of Coxwold is Byland Abbey, one of the most picturesque monastic sites in the whole of Yorkshire. The great hanging semi-circle of the west front, which a twenty-six foot diameter wheel window once occupied, is visible from afar; purity of line combines with the brutal fact of ruination to ensure its shape lingers in the mind.

The story of Byland began in 1134 when monks from Furness Abbey attempted to make a new settlement first in Cumberland

A medieval tile pavement in the south transept chapel of Byland Abbey. The mosaic pavements were originally brightly coloured; green and yellow were two of the most commonly-used glazes.

and then near Thirsk. They outgrew their Yorkshire home and moved to Old Byland (just west of Rievaulx Abbey) in 1143, but the close proximity of the older foundation caused difficulties and a further move in 1147 took the monks five miles south, close to the eventual site of Byland Abbey.

By this time the foundation, originally Savigniac, had been absorbed by the Cistercians, and their first small monastery was built a mile and a half to the west of Byland.

Meanwhile the marshy land at Byland was drained, and work began on building the new monastery; some buildings were habitable by 1177. As the abbey prospered so construction continued, and the final stages of the church were finished in 1225.

A setback for the monks occurred in 1322 when the abbey was raided by the Scots, but although the number of monks declined

The medieval tile pavement at Byland Abbey, showing (top right) brighter, less worn tiles on the riser.

The picturesque ruins of Byland Abbey, a Cistercian foundation dating from the twelfth century.

towards the end of the fourteenth century, by the time of its dissolution in 1538 the foundation had once more become a thriving concern.

Much of the west front and the north wall of the 330 foot long church remains standing, and in the transept chapels are fine examples of the mosaic tile pavements which originally covered the entire floor of the church. The rich green and yellow glazes are still visible on many tiles, and their natural variation in colour adds a splendid subtlety to the geometric patterns. The surface of the tiles which front the steps has never been worn away, and the colour of these risers shows how bright the church would have been in the mid-thirteenth century.

The lie of the land allowed the monastic buildings to be set out in an almost ideal Cistercian formation, and enough remains of the large cloister and other offices to enable the ground plan to be easily discerned.

From Byland, a circuitous journey will take the traveller westward towards Thirsk, first visiting the tiny church of St Mary at Birdforth, right beside the A19; the route lies back through Coxwold and on to Carlton Husthwaite, before joining the trunk road half a mile north of Birdforth.

The simple, rubblestone church has a pantiled roof and dates from Norman times or possibly earlier. Its attraction stems from the contrast with its surroundings as much from any intrinsic architectural qualities.

At Thirkleby, three miles north of Birdforth (up the A19 then right to the village), another eccentric E B Lamb church may be found. All Saints, built in 1850, is a wilfully asymmetrical composition which hides a good hammerbeam roof.

Cross the A19 and head west to Dalton, caught between the east coast main railway line and the A1, just four miles south of Thirsk. Look inside the church of St John the Evangelist to see unexpected colour, for this is a design by William Butterfield, carried out in 1868. The nave has bands of stone and blue brick intermingled with red, there are tile patterns in the chancel, and the glass is by William Morris.

Butterfield was a master of polychromy, and used colour and variety in materials to emphasise the structural features of his works. His career stretched from the late 1830s until the 1870s, and churches formed the bulk of his output; his series of small Yorkshire churches is particularly delightful, as each is a completely individual design, produced with a specific location and local materials in mind.

The friendly market town of Thirsk beckons from the north; those arriving by train are treated to a mile walk into the centre, as the station is west of the town, but the racecourse and its grandstand provide a diverting spectacle along the way.

Market Place is emphatically at the heart of Thirsk and rarely seems quiet; the town had aspirations to spa status as well as being an important post and coaching point in the eighteenth and early nineteenth centuries, and thus has the requisite number of inns dotted about its centre. The Fleece Hotel, parading a pretty Gothick bay window on its Georgian façade, was the main coaching inn, but the Three Tuns is the oldest inn, and was once the town's manor house.

The church of St Mary in Kirkgate, north of Market Place, is the outstanding specimen of Perpendicular church architecture in the North Riding. It originated with the founding of a chantry chapel by Robert Thirsk, who died in 1419, and building probably began around 1430 and continued into the early sixteenth century. Openwork battlements march along the top of every available outer wall, giving a martial first impression of the exterior, soon corrected when the elegance of the tracery in the tall clerestory windows becomes apparent. Inside, a few elements are due to a restoration of 1877, but most is true Perpendicular.

Leave Thirsk behind to travel west along the Ripon road (A61) and cross the river Swale at Skipton-on-Swale, via the eight arch bridge built by John Carr in 1781. Although the Swale does not appear much of a barrier at this point, bridges are few in the vale, and the next most northerly is nine miles away on the A684 to the west of Northallerton.

For a more oblique exit from Thirsk, take the road leading north-west from beside the racecourse. This passes the wonderful ironwork gates of Thornton-le-Street Hall (the eighteenth century hall has been demolished) before joining the A167.

Half a mile north is the turning for Kirby Wiske, where the church of St John the Baptist holds two interesting oddments: an Easter Sepulchre, which held the sacrament and crucifix before Easter; and a white marble and bronze monument to one Mrs Samuelson, who died in 1898. The latter was designed in 1900 by Sir George Frampton, sculptor of Peter Pan in London's Kensington Gardens, and shows the good lady with her children.

On through Kirby Wiske to reach the Swale at Maunby, but here we may only look across to the far bank, as there is no bridge. Once, trains on the Northallerton to Ripon railway line were whisked over the river on a viaduct, but the line is no more, so head back to the south and over the river on the A61 at Skipton-on-Swale, looking for a heavenly spire.

Only three miles away at Baldersby St James (turn off the A61 a mile south of Baldersby) is the church of St James the Greater, designed by William Butterfield in 1855-7, with a 160 foot high spire which is visible for miles around.

In fact Butterfield built most of the tiny village for Viscount Downe of Baldersby Park, the elegant Palladian mansion which stands a couple of miles east of the village. It was designed by Colen Campbell in 1720-8, and was one of the first few Palladian revival houses in the country.

Viscount Downe was a frequent patron of Butterfield, financing several Yorkshire churches, and for Baldersby village his architect produced a rather Germanic effect especially noticeable in the school, which has a high and steeply-pitched roof. The red-roofed church is large enough for a small town, and has a lavishly equipped and colourful interior; pink brick and white stone alternate in the nave, while the chancel is lined with alabaster panelling. Viscount Downe died soon after laying the first stone of his new church; his memorial stands in the chancel, now an integral part of the building which is the culmination of his patronage.

Reverting to the A61, cross the A1 and after a mile cut off to the north via Melmerby to Wath, where the late medieval manor house Norton Conyers may be found to the south of the village.

The earliest remaining parts of the house date from the mid-fourteenth century; during rebuilding around 1500, the façade of the plain, brick house was enlivened by battlements, and the house was again rebuilt in the early seventeenth century. York architect

An early Edwardian view of Norton Conyers, a much-rebuilt late medieval manor house.

Above: the spire of St James the Greater at Baldersby St James, built by William Butterfield for Viscount Downe of nearby Baldersby Park in 1855-7.

Top: the North and West Ridings meet on the bridge over the River Ure at West Tanfield, which was built around 1734; and (bottom) a stone dog-tether waits patiently outside the medieval church of St Nicholas.

William Belwood, who worked for Robert Adam at Harewood House, made further alterations and added the stables in 1780-6. The four great gables of the west façade, dating from the seventeenth century, are the most memorable features of its exterior.

Follow the road west from Wath to find the West Riding border at West Tanfield marked by two extremely weathered but still readable plaques on the bridge across the Ure, which was built around 1734. The village church, St Nicholas, is prettily sited above the river, and

The fifteenth century Marmion Tower (left) is all that remains of the castle which once stood beside the Ure at West Tanfield; the church of St Nicholas is to its right.

for worshipping dog-owners has stone dog-tethers outside the porch. The Marmion Chapel holds effigies of assorted members of the Marmion family and their hounds. The Marmion Tower, a gatehouse which is the only surviving part of the family castle built in the early fifteenth century, stands just a few yards from the church. A delicate oriel window looks out over the Ure from the first floor of the tower.

Journey a couple of miles north from West Tanfield along the byroad which leads eventually to Bedale, but initially to the village of Well, perched on the hillside, where the medieval church of St Michael takes us back several more centuries, as it is home to a mosaic pavement moved from a nearby Roman villa.

A little further towards Bedale and just east of the road is Snape, with the imposing ruins of a four-towered medieval castle, and then Thorp Perrow, where part of the estate has been planted as an arboretum. The elegant Classical house at Thorp Perrow was built around 1802, and designed by Richmond mason and self-taught architect John Foss.

Bedale is only two miles on, via the B6268; the north end of its long and gently curving Market Place is dominated by the tower of St Gregory's Church, a thirteenth or fourteenth century addition to an older building. Close by is Bedale Hall, although its main façade, in stone and dating from around 1730, looks away from the town and has the appearance of a country house.

Leave Bedale by the A684 to find the pleasantly picturesque village of Great Crakehall two miles to the north-west. Here a Victorian church, early eighteenth century

Crakehall Hall and the village green combine with handily-sited trees to good effect. Just across Crakehall Beck in Little Crakehall is a restored watermill, originally part of the estate of Middleham Castle in the fifteenth century. It was a working corn mill complete with three pairs of millstones until 1927, and was restored in the late 1970s. The seventeenth century building now houses eighteenth and nineteenth century machinery.

To cross the Swale once more, head north from Little Crakehall through Hackforth to Catterick, an important coaching point on the Great North Road but now bypassed — although only just — by the A1, which travels high above the Swale a mile north of the village at Catterick Bridge. The Roman settlement of Cataractonium, which gave Catterick its name, lay to the north-west of the present village. The rebuilding of the church of St Anne may be dated exactly to 1412-15 by the contract between the mason, Richard of Crakehall, and the clients, members of the de Burgh family, whose monuments may be found within; the fine black marble font is also in the Perpendicular style, and adorned with heraldic carving.

The de Burgh family was also responsible for the building of Catterick Bridge in 1422, although this has been much altered. Their home was Brough Hall, just over a mile to the west of the river crossing (off the A6136 road to Catterick Garrison); it was then a simple tower-house, but Elizabethan work combined with a near-rebuilding around 1725 and again in the 1770s resulted in what appears to be a completely Classical country house faced in pink sandstone. It has now been converted into housing.

The watermill at Little Crakehall is a seventeenth century structure, containing machinery dating from the eighteenth and nineteenth centuries. It stopped working around 1927, but corn-grinding began again in 1980, after restoration.

This obelisk, erected in 1743 in the churchyard of St Mary at Bolton-on-Swale, commemorates the long life of Henry Jenkins.

Cross over the Swale and head east for two miles, via the B6271 or the riverside path, to Bolton-on-Swale where the church of St Mary harbours all manner of surprises. First, in the churchyard stands a hefty obelisk with a knobbly finial commemorating one Henry Jenkins, a local lad born in 1500 who reached

the age of 169 before he died in 1670. Remarkable indeed, and for some unaccountable reason his monument was not erected until 1743. He has another memorial inside the church, which itself dates from the fourteenth century, although the west tower is two centuries younger. Henry Jenkins doubtless watched its construction.

Architect William Eden Nesfield worked at St Mary in 1877. He was one of the main forces behind the popularity of the Queen Anne Revival style in the late nineteenth century; it was a style which threw off the Gothic connection between decoration and construction, and allowed and encouraged ornament for its own sake.

At St Mary, he added a dado of Spanish-style cuenca tiles — featuring high-relief geometric patterns with green, purple, orange and white glazes — to the chancel and the Carpenter Chapel. These colourful tiles were then a fashionable feature of chancel decoration, replicating Moorish work on Christian churches in Spain. The Carpenter Chapel also has an unusual sculpted plasterwork frieze dating from 1905, which shows farming and seafaring scenes. Altogether St Mary, in its pleasing rural situation, is a church not to be missed.

Northallerton lies east along the winding B6271 past Kiplin Hall, which was built about 1625 to a plan of a square over a cross, a rather late example of the Elizabethan fashion for and enjoyment of pure pattern.

The traveller then arrives at that rarity, a bridge across the Swale at Great Langton. The tiny twelfth century village church stands to the south beside the river, on the road to late Georgian Langton Hall.

Five miles further is Yafforth, where a Norman castle once stood on Howe Hill to the north of the village, by the River Wiske. Following the Wiske three miles upstream on the byroad north of Yafforth will reveal more evidence of the Normans at Danby Wiske, where the tympanum above the south door of the church is Norman work. It is the only remaining North Riding tympanum of this date still in its original position, but is not an impressive piece.

And so to Northallerton, capital of the Riding and busy market town. The overall feeling of High Street and the market place is Georgian, although the town hall dates from 1873 and County Hall is twentieth century.

The latter is the work of the North Riding's official architect between 1901 and 1923, Walter Brierley, the son of a York architect. His County Hall was built in 1904-6 in his favourite style for public buildings, combining brick with decorative stone dressings in what came to be called the Wrenaissance idiom, after Christopher Wren's adaptations of European Renaissance style. Brierley built widely throughout Yorkshire from the 1890s until the 1920s, using the Arts and Crafts style for country houses and Gothic for churches. This stylistic eclecticism was then seen as necessarily practical, rather than as a sign of theoretical incompetence.

Leave Northallerton on the Darlington road (A167), passing All Saints Church brooding over the north end of High Street, to find, only three miles north, the site of the Battle of the Standard, which took place on the 22nd August 1138. This confrontation between Scots and English interests formed part of the resolution of the disputed succession to the throne after the death of Henry I in 1135. Although the English won the battle, the war continued and the Scots retreated to wreak havoc in the borders. The battlefield was just east of the A167, and the position of the English lines is marked by a monument at the roadside, half a mile before the Oaktree Hill crossroad.

Only six miles to the north is County Durham, the border delineated by the meandering Tees which cuts great curving swathes through the peaceful landscape. This is odd country; the search for a bridge may take the traveller many miles along narrow, verdant roads, up and down steep river cliffs and generally out of the way. It is easy to forget that Middlesbrough and Darlington are a mere few miles distant.

The A167 crosses the Tees at Croft, but turn east on a byroad at Great Smeaton to visit East Rounton (six miles via Hornby and Appleton Wiske), where the village school (now a house) was built by Philip Webb for Middlesbrough ironmaster Isaac Lowthian Bell in 1876. Bell bought the East Rounton estate in 1870, and commissioned Webb to design a family house. Rounton Grange, a rambling neo-Georgian mansion on a tower house theme, was built in 1872-6, and allowed Webb to use a variety of English imagery in an idiosyncratic and influential manner. Sadly the house, designed for an era when servants were plentiful, was demolished in 1954.

But all is not lost, as Webb's Smeaton Manor, built for Bell's son-in-law in 1876-9, stands just to the west of Great Smeaton; the byroad to East Cowton passes the site soon after the village. The house was designed in an inventive reworking of neo-Georgian, which was part of the late nineteenth century search by Webb and other architects for an essentially English style.

Follow the lane west past Smeaton Manor to East Cowton and then North Cowton; South Cowton exists only in the form of the solitary church of St Mary standing in fields off the B1263. A footpath leads from the road half a mile south of North Cowton, heading for the church via Atley Fields Farm. Looking south from the lonely churchyard, a castle may be seen on the horizon; this is Cowton Castle, a late fifteenth century tower-house built by Sir Richard Conyers, who also responsible for the church. St Mary was built around 1450-70 and inside, under the fine roof, are equally fine contemporary wall-paintings, and a good screen and choir stalls.

The village of Moulton, four miles west of North Cowton, boasts two excellent seventeenth century houses, both built by members of the Smithson family; a Smithson from another branch of the family later became the first Duke of Northumberland.

Moulton Manor, in the centre of the village, was built about 1570 and much altered in the earlier part of the seventeenth century. The three storey house was erected on an H-shape plan using rubblestone, with the main entrance in the centre of a three-bay recess. Moulton Hall stands a little to the south of the village. It was built soon after 1654, and the exterior is given a theatrical air by the five Dutch gables pointing skyward above the second storey. The main staircase is a riot of flowery woodcarving.

For a glimpse of a spa town which never quite reached its potential, head seven miles north-east from Moulton through Middleton Tyas, to the village of Croft-on-Tees. It once had aspirations to be a spa on the scale of Harrogate, but eventually had to settle for the steadier income gained by catering for post and coach services using the Great North Road, which crossed the Tees at Croft Bridge.

The Croft springs had been known from around 1689 and bottled water from the Old Well was on sale in London by 1713, but the lack of suitable lodgings in the village discouraged visitors, and by the late eighteenth century the coaching trade had become more important than exploitation of the waters.

In the early nineteenth century the opening of the New Well kindled a renewed burst of interest in the waters, and the Croft Spa Hotel, on the west of the A167, was built in 1835. It was financed by lord of the manor Sir William Chaytor, whose ancestors had failed to invest in the development of Croft as a spa in the early eighteenth century. He chose for his architect Ignatius Bonomi of Durham, who produced a gentle Classical design for the hotel; he later built a Romanesque-style mansion for Sir William. Bonomi also designed the pretty, verandahed Spa Buildings, sited just south of the village, in 1835 but this was demolished some time ago.

Croft as a spa flourished during the mid-nineteenth century, but the delights of Harrogate were tough competition for the little village spa, and it was in decline by 1890. Today Croft remains small, dwarfed by neighbouring Hurworth across the Tees, which is a commuter suburb for Darlington.

The most striking feature of Croft is the red sandstone church of St Peter, sited right beside Croft Bridge. The church is partly Norman, but its present appearance is mainly a result

*Above left: the isolated church of St Mary at South Cowton was built in the
fifteenth century by Sir Richard Conyers, whose castle stands
just to the south.*

*Above right: inside the west end of St John the Baptist, near Stanwick-St-
John. The church, which dates from the Norman period, was heavily restored
by Anthony Salvin in 1868.*

*Right: approaching Bolton-on-Swale from the west, across
the agricultural plain created by the River Swale.*

of twelfth to fifteenth century alterations and additions. The relatively unassuming exterior does not prepare the visitor for the sight of the Milbanke family pew, which dominates the interior. The Milbankes lived at Halnaby Hall, a splendid mansion dating from the seventeenth and eighteenth centuries which stood three miles south-west of Croft, just south of the road from Middleton Tyas. It was demolished in 1952, although several of the service buildings still remain. The flamboyant late seventeenth century Milbanke pew is hoisted above the floor of the church on Tuscan columns, allowing the family to ascend the long and decorative staircase to watch over parishoners and parson from the comfort of their private box.

Travelling west from Middleton Tyas, the byroad passes the entrance to Middleton Lodge, a country house designed by John Carr in 1777-80, before negotiating the A1, an unexpected and unwelcome intrusion into this peaceful countryside. Onwards through Melsonby, where the church stands high above the village street, to meet the B6274 and turn north to Forcett.

Here the dramatic triumphal gateway of Forcett Park separates villagers from the grounds of Forcett Hall, rebuilt around 1730-40 for Richard Shuttleworth by Daniel Garrett — well-known in the north of England for his country-house work — in the Palladian style propounded by Lord Burlington. At Forcett, Garrett designed a straightforward seven-bay main block, pedimented and faced in sandstone, with a set of Ionic pilasters for the garden front.

At the edge of the park stands an elegant, mid-eighteenth century, hexagonal sandstone dovecot, which may be seen from the road. At its base is an open arcade, while a tiny colonnaded cupola hovers above the slate roof. The nest boxes shelter inside the upper storey. An ice-house, grotto and walled garden also remain in the park, while the village church, St Cuthbert, can boast various Shuttleworth memorials and fine mid-nineteenth century furniture.

But what of the strange landforms beside the byroad leading immediately east from the park gates towards Stanwick-St-John? Almost as far as the eye can see, the meadows roll and surge in distinctly odd shapes, surely the work of human hands. Indeed, these are the Stanwick Fortifications, a huge complex of earthworks stretching for over six miles and 850 acres. The earth and stone banks were built by the Brigantes as part of their resistance to Roman occupation in the middle years of the first century.

An excavated section of the fortifications may be seen in Forcett village, but the minor road south to the church of St John the Baptist, near Stanwick village, takes the traveller into the centre of the system of banks and ditches. The church stands amidst a screen of yew trees surrounded by the billowing banks in a calm and peaceful spot beside a stream, although amazingly it is merely three or four miles distant from the A1. St John dates from Norman times, but a thorough restoration in 1868 accounts for its Victorian looks, exemplified by the green and purple tiles lining the reredos.

Inside the church are monuments to members of the local Smithson family; Sir Hugh Smithson married the daughter of the Earl of Northumberland in 1740, and eventually became duke in his own right. It was the Duchess of Northumberland who employed Anthony Salvin, pupil of John Nash and best known for his country-house work, to carry out the rebuilding of St John.

The church in its setting contrives to encapsulate an outline of English history from Roman times to the present day. The fact that the church is now redundant reflects the continued evolution of the site, from martial to ecclesiastical and now perhaps to secular; fortunately for the serenity of St John, isolation is no great crowd-puller.

GOTHICK GEMS AND A PLUNDERED DALE

Richmond, Swaledale and the North

IDYLLICALLY SITUATED beside the River Swale and only a mile from Richmond, Easby Abbey is the perfect introduction to an exploration of Swaledale. The refectory walls still stand high enough to enclose a series of huge windows, and even the delicate tracery of the east window has survived; this is a picturesque sight rising ahead on the path from Richmond.

Roald, constable of Richmond Castle, founded the abbey around 1155. The later involvement at Easby of Richard, Lord Scrope, one of the most powerful men in fourteenth century England, makes the abbey a singular appetiser for the buildings of Swaledale.

Easby Abbey was a Premonstratensian foundation; this was a relatively puritanical order of canons which originated in France and began to spead rapidly throughout England from 1143. Premonstratensian abbeys tended to be located in remote spots.

The Easby canons soon began to take an interest in sheep farming, acquiring pasture-land on sites to the north of Richmond and in Wensleydale. In the fourteenth century, the abbey was severely damaged by Scottish and English soldiers during bouts of border warfare, but was further endowed in 1392-3 by Richard, Lord Scrope. Scrope, who became Lord High Chancellor of England in 1379 and whose home was Bolton Castle in Wensley-dale, funded extra canons and a hospital for the poor. By the end of the fourteenth century, Easby was home to around thirty canons, but the number had halved by the time of the abbey's dissolution in 1537.

The single most imposing element in the ruins of the abbey is the refectory or frater, standing two stories high to the south of the site. Its lower floor was used mostly for storage, while canons ate on the upper floor, lit by the magnificent windows. To the west and close to the Swale is another substantial remnant, consisting of the guest house and lavatories; the position of the building, near the river, was dictated by drainage needs.

The abbey church barely survives above ground, but the parish church of St Agatha,

The interior of the refectory at Easby Abbey, near Richmond. The lower floor of this two-storey structure was used for storage, while the refectory occupied the upper floor.

The temptation of Adam in the Garden of Eden; one of the late thirteenth century wall-paintings in the church of St Agatha, Easby.

which dates from before the foundation of the abbey, is still intact just south of the refectory. The original church was erected between 1086 and 1155, and sections of the Easby Cross, an early ninth century cross with superb carving, were used as building stone. The Anglo-Saxon cross now resides in the Victoria and Albert Museum, but a cast does duty inside the church. St Agatha was enlarged around 1200, with thirteenth and fourteenth century additions of transepts and a south aisle; restoration in 1869 was by Sir George Gilbert Scott. Apart from the cross, the interior holds excellent late thirteenth century wall-paintings. Figures in contemporary dress act out scenes from the Garden of Eden and the life of Christ.

Either a pleasant riverside footpath or the B6271 will take the traveller from Easby to Richmond, a town of huge architectural interest in a wonderfully picturesque setting.

Although there were settlements all around, Richmond, as such, did not exist before the arrival of the Normans. Earl Alan the Red, leader of the Bretons at the battle of Hastings, was given the estates, which became known as the Honour of Richmond, as a reward for his part in the harrying of the North in 1069-70. He began the construction of Richmond Castle, on its commanding site above the Swale, around 1071.

Timber-framed houses were built, at first within the inner bailey of the castle, and then on plots of land to its north and east, and the town thrived. It became an important trade centre for the surrounding area by the end of the twelfth century, gained a general market by 1268, and — despite fourteenth century depression — grew to a population of around 620 by 1377.

Richmond survived the economically difficult fifteenth century, and was again expanding at the end of the sixteenth century. Agriculture and textiles, mainly woollens, were at the source of the town's prosperity, which reached its zenith in the Georgian period, when Richmond was also an administrative and legal centre of high provincial status. The social whirl consequent upon this cultural role produced an assortment of entertainments, from horseracing to the theatre, and was important to the town in architectural and financial terms.

The railway arrived at Richmond in 1846, but the station was a terminus, apt for a town whose development seems, happily perhaps, to have been arrested in the nineteenth century. No railway ever ran through Swaledale, although schemes were put forward for this costly exercise from the 1840s until just before the First World War. The Richmond line cut the cost of transporting lead from the Swaledale mines to Stockton by around a third, and in any case a Swaledale line would have found leadmining, the dale's main industry, in decline from the 1870s. Twentieth century Richmond is something of a commuter town, but acts as a springboard for Swaledale tourism and still retains its service function in relation to nearby Catterick Garrison.

At the centre of Richmond is Market Place, a roughly rectangular space with gently curving sides. It slopes from west down to east, and at first glance has an overwhelmingly eighteenth century appearance, although several of the shops are nineteenth century or later. The Georgian era saw the small-scale shops of medieval Richmond swept away; the upper stories of their replacements are still visible above the modern façades. The whole is particularly pleasing, although no one element stands out, except the Obelisk, at the higher, western, end of Market Place. It is a Georgian replacement for the market cross, and is sited above an underground reservoir

Morris-dancers gathered around the Obelisk in Richmond Market Place. The tapering column replaced an older market cross in 1771.

which provided water to the public founts in the town. The slightly obese column was erected in 1771 by Christopher Wayne, then mayor of the town.

The centre of Market Place is filled by Holy Trinity, originally a chapel but now a regimental museum, and a group of shops clustered around its eastern extremity. The

Richmond Castle, built largely in the late eleventh century, stands on the north bank of the River Swale.

court and warehouse, but sadly its appearance is rather less exciting than its history. Internally, most features date from the 1864 restoration in Gothic style.

On the southern edge of Market Place is the town hall, built around 1756, the first of Richmond's Georgian public buildings. Just to its east is the airy market hall of 1854, its stone exterior concealing cast iron columns within. Head back, past the town hall and obelisk, to leave Market Place at its south-west corner, turning sharply left to find the lofty and impressive ruins of the castle.

Despite its size — the sandstone keep still climbs to over 100 feet in height — the castle does not dominate the town, except in the picturesque views from paths along the far bank of the Swale. The river protected the site on two sides, and the remainder was defended by the massive walls of the inner bailey, which enclosed the living quarters.

Initially, the castle took about twenty years to build, from around 1071, and Alan the Red incorporated several unusual features into the structure: it was stone-built, when other castles were still being constructed of timber; towers projected from the walls to improve the defences; and the great hall, named Scolland's Hall after Alan's steward, was the earliest of its type in England.

The keep was a later addition, built in the third quarter of the twelfth century by Conan the Little, Earl of Richmond and great-nephew of Alan the Red. It is sited above the original gatehouse, on the town side of the castle. The keep was purely a military structure, an integral part of the castle's defences, without the domestic accommodation usually found in Norman keeps.

chapel is a most peculiar building; it was founded around 1135, and fragments of the tower are twelfth century. However, much has been altered, and now the tower is connected to the church by an office building, and the church itself is on an upper floor. Very strange. Apart from its religious function, Holy Trinity has served as a prison, school,

So effective were the defences in deterring attackers and emphasising Norman dominance that the castle led a largely peaceful existence. By the fourteenth century the structure had gone into decline, and was said to be in need of repair, and by the mid-sixteenth century it was a ruin.

The castle returned to military use in the mid-nineteenth century, but perhaps its finest hour was the Georgian era, when its picturesque beauty was appreciated to the full by visitors promenading along Castle Walk, between the river and the southern walls.

Today, we can also look out at the town from the castle keep; all around is a complex jumble of red-pantiled and slate roofs, and a network of narrow alleys on different levels. Richmond is largely a stone-built town, although this implies no uniformity, as the stone came from at least four different sources: there were tough grey and brown limestones, a more workable sandstone and cobbles from the bed of the Swale, again mostly sandstone. The ubiquitous pantiles — large tiles with an S-shaped cross-section — first appeared in England during the seventeenth century; the Richmond pantiles were probably made in Boroughbridge or Darlington.

West of the castle, across Bridge Street (leading to the 1788 bridge by John Carr), is the Green, which originated as an industrial suburb of medieval Richmond, complete with tanneries, mills and a brewery. Now it is more a picturesque epilogue to the town, and the walls to its west hide Richmond's Gothick gem, the Culloden Tower. For a view of this elegant architectural confection, either climb the castle keep, or cross the Swale and take the

The Culloden Tower, political statement and garden building, as seen from Richmond Castle. The tower was built in 1746-7, and is now a holiday home.

path west through the woods, and all will be revealed.

The octagonal, two-storey tower stands on a square base (originally a barn) sited high above the river. A pinnacled, openwork parapet and a domed turret (above a spiral staircase) complete the tower. Inside are two tall, octagonal rooms, both with fireplaces;

the Gothick lower room is all pointed, plaster arches and rich carving, while the upper room is Rococo in style.

But how did this Gothick essay come to pass in restrained, Georgian Richmond? The Culloden Tower stands in the grounds of Yorke House, built in the latter part of the seventeenth century as the home of the Yorke family. The Yorkes allied themselves with the Darcy family, Richmond landowners, in local battles for political power in the early eighteenth century, and both factions represented Richmond in parliament, although they were later to disagree. The marital alliance of John Yorke and Anne Darcy built the Culloden Tower in the grounds of their home in 1746-7, marking the victory of the Hanoverian Duke of Cumberland, whose troops included the Yorke's son Joseph, over the Jacobites at Culloden. The Hanoverians were thus confirmed in power, and for the Whig couple all was well with the world.

The architect of their celebratory tower was probably Daniel Garrett, or perhaps William Kent, both of whom had already worked for Anne's father at Aske Hall, north of Richmond. Garrett executed the final design for the Temple, a garden building at Aske Hall, after initial sketches by the inventive Kent. Garrett was once clerk of works to Lord Burlington, and designed fashionable Palladian country houses, although he also specialised in farm buildings, in the age of agricultural improvement, and produced occasional Gothick oddments with Rococo decoration.

Apart from its political symbolism, the Culloden Tower was simply a garden building, used, perhaps, for summer meals and observing the excellent view. It eventually fell into disrepair and was in a sad state by the 1970s, but restoration was carried out in 1982 by the Landmark Trust, and the tower is now a holiday home.

Yorke House was demolished in 1821, but Temple Lodge, erected in 1769 by Thomas Yorke, still stands in the Yorke parkland just off Cravengate, which runs north of the Green.

The fifteenth century Greyfriars Tower in Richmond was part of the church of a Franciscan foundation. Nothing more remains of their buildings.

In its original Gothick form it was built as a menagerie — Georgian home-entertainment? — but the castellations result from mid-nineteenth century enlargements.

Further north along Cravengate, a right turn, opposite the elegant original gateway to the Culloden Tower, takes the walker into handsome, largely eighteenth century Newbiggin, one of the town's best streets. At its end turn left, then right into Victoria Road, where an exciting trio of buildings awaits.

Most obvious, on the north side of Victoria Road, is Greyfriars Tower, the sole remnant above ground of a friary founded in 1258. The Franciscan's early buildings were unexceptional, but the sandstone tower, which stood between nave and chancel, dates from a late fifteenth century rebuilding and has an attractive openwork parapet.

Across the road is Richmond's most intriguing building, the Georgian Theatre Royal. It is totally unremarkable from the outside, but the interior is a small but authentic Georgian theatre, the best example in England. Boxes on two levels line the side walls of the auditorium, and the proscenium is only 18 feet wide and 20 feet high. The atmosphere is intimate and unique.

The theatre was built in 1788 by Samuel Butler, whose company of travelling players worked a Northern circuit including most of Yorkshire. They visited Richmond regularly from at least 1774, and after parliament passed an act in 1788 legalising provincial dramatic performances, Butler took the opportunity to develop his own theatre in the town. The theatre season was September and October, which partly coincided with Richmond's popular horserace meeting, and the Theatre Royal thrived for the first two decades or so of its life.

However, after Butler's death in 1812 the theatre company declined, although performances continued until 1830. The theatre was empty until 1848, when it was let out as a wine vault and auction rooms; the first suggestions of restoration came in 1943, but the process was not completed for twenty years. Necessary additions were made in keeping with the original structure, and a performance can now transport the audience back to Georgian times. Indeed, the almost halved official capacity of the theatre — well down from the original 450 — is perhaps the most noticeable difference between the eighteenth and twentieth century theatres.

Next door to the theatre is the third in the trio of oddball buildings, a towering and theatrical pub, the Fleece Hotel. A Richmond castle in miniature, the pub is faced in red brick and gaudy yellow terracotta, and topped by turrets springing out from the walls. This wonderfully jolly, if a little heavy-handed, Scottish Baronial transplant was designed in 1897 by Darlington architect G G Hoskins, who was also responsible for Middlesbrough Town Hall. His designs were normally fairly flamboyant, and as the Fleece was a public house rather than a more serious building, he clearly felt free to produce a fun façade.

Stroll on eastward, past the junction with King Street and along narrow Ryders Wynd, then left on to the cobbles of Frenchgate, Richmond's first suburb, with its fine collection of Georgian town-houses and splendid doorcases. Halfway up the hill, take Church Wynd on the right to find the parish church of St Mary.

Most appears Victorian on the outside, and indeed this is the work of George Gilbert Scott, who restored St Mary in 1859-60. But there has been a church on this site since 1135 and possibly before, and elements of the interior date from the twelfth century. It must be said that the church monuments and furniture are more interesting than the fabric of St Mary; the choir stalls came from Easby Abbey, just before its dissolution, and have jovial carvings on the misericords. Look out for the dancing pigs!

The churchyard leads on to Station Road, which takes you across the Swale to the station, now a garden centre, but happily retaining its glazed trainshed. Architect G T Andrews normally produced Classical stations, but for Richmond, opened by the Great North of England Railway in 1846, he chose Jacobethan, in an attempt to blend in with the fabric of the town. There are tall chimneys, a hefty *porte cochere* and mullioned windows, the whole in local sandstone. The ironwork was by John Walker of York, later the royal ironfounder. The station was closed in 1969.

Richmond Station was built on the site of a water mill owned by St Martin's Priory, the ruins of which lie just to the south-east. The Benedictine priory was founded in 1100, and the visible remains — a gatehouse and part of a church — date mainly from the fifteenth century, although there is also a twelfth century doorway.

Much more may be explored in Richmond, but Swaledale beckons, so head north from the town, up and out, on the old road to Marske, Hurgill Road (off Victoria Road). In a mile, just to the north of the road, is the site of Richmond Racecourse, now a windswept

A jolly grotesque ornaments Richmond's old railway station, which was built by G T Andrews for the Great North of England Railway in 1846.

gallops with a huge and expansive view which stretches as far as Middlesbrough to the north-east.

Racing first took place on High Moor around 1576, and became increasingly popular with the local gentry; from 1759 assemblies were run in the town hall to coincide with race week, and in 1765 the course was moved to an

The judge's box at Richmond Racecourse, where horseracing took place between 1765 and the end of the nineteenth century. In the background is the old grandstand, built around 1776.

improved site. An elegant two-storey sandstone grandstand was erected around 1776. Spectators viewed the races from a balcony supported by Tuscan columns and edged by wrought iron railings. Race meetings ceased towards the end of the nineteenth century, but the sad remains of the grandstand survive, as does the restored judge's box, a small stone building provided with a bow window; this dates from 1814.

The tiny village of Marske is sited in the valley of Marske Beck, and visited by hundreds of walkers every summer due to its position on the Coast to Coast trail across the North of England. Indeed, Swaledale has paths galore, and an ample supply of river bridges, making exploration of the dale, whether by the main B6270 or by-roads, a simple task.

Marske is dominated by the combination of church and hall, separated by the beck and the ornamental gardens of Marske Hall. The hall was built by the Hutton family, who bought the Marske estate in 1597 and soon began to rebuild the existing hall, probably to a design by — or at least influenced by — Robert Smythson. Only a small part of this structure remains, as much of the hall was rebuilt around 1730, leaving us a rather dull exterior.

More interesting is the garden by the beck, which was laid out with a pond and Classical arcade after a new turnpike road ran through the grounds of the hall in the late 1830s.

The church of St Edmund King and Martyr, overlooking this delightful and unexpected garden, dates from around 1090 but has been much altered, generally at the behest of the Huttons. Restoration in 1683 left the church with two peculiar nave windows on the south side, which seem to be seventeenth century attempts to copy Norman and Gothic work. Inside are box pews and a large family pew.

The road south from Marske leads across the Swale at Downholme Bridge, but look back to see Hutton's Monument high on the hill to the west. This unattainable sandstone obelisk was erected in the family deer park to commemorate Matthew Hutton, who died in 1814.

Once over the Swale the road meets the A6108, and continues south past the church of St Michael, sited above the road and well to the north of its village, Downholme, which is now much smaller than in its leadworking days. The prettily-sited church dates from the twelfth century, but with many later alterations.

Nearly two miles further south, on a sharp bend in the road, is Walburn Hall, a fortified manor house built in the late fifteenth and sixteenth centuries, and later sold to the Hutton family. A battlemented wall screens the courtyard from the road, and the house, with its mullioned windows and oriels, is a typically Elizabethan composition. The substantial chimney at the rear might have been part of the brewhouse.

Reeth, Swaledale's major village, may be reached via north or south bank, but the minor road west from Marske allows a detour to Marrick, where a stroll down towards the Swale along a pleasant, wooded lane leads to Marrick Priory. This house of Benedictine nuns was founded in the mid-twelfth century. What remains is the church of St Andrew, which was largely rebuilt in 1811, became a ruin, then was converted in the late 1960s to educational use. It is a romantic setting but the buildings are a little disappointing, with only the late fifteenth century west tower of the church easily visible. A second nunnery — this time Cistercian — stood over the river and half a mile to the east at Ellerton Abbey, but little remains except the fifteenth century tower of the priory church.

Grinton stands a mile south-east of Reeth on the main Swaledale road, and is home to the church of St Andrew, the parish church of the upper part of the dale, a huge area. St Andrew, often known as the Cathedral of the Dales, was built and extended in the twelfth to sixteenth centuries, but the long, low church looks mainly Perpendicular.

A pleasant walk, over Grinton Bridge and left across the meadows, leads to Reeth, passing an impressive breastshot waterwheel at Fremington corn mill, a late eighteenth century building. Reeth then lies on the far side of Arkle Beck, over Reeth Bridge, a John Carr construction of 1773.

Reeth is tidily laid out around a large green, its most prestigious buildings lining the west side, High Row, although the best of them is the mid-eighteenth century Burgoyne Hotel, on the higher, northern side. Reeth was a market town from the seventeenth century, but leadmining in adjacent Arkengarthdale, the valley of Arkle Beck, brought additional prosperity in the eighteenth century, and thus the unusually urban style of architecture.

The road north from Reeth leads up Arkengarthdale and gives splendid views over the narrow valley, which has more visible signs of leadmining than any other dale, although the industry was of great importance in Swaledale and the dales to the south.

Lead was mined in the area as early as the Iron Age, but by the eighteenth century outside investors, rather than working miners, were beginning to take over mineral rights. The new proprietors began mining on a significantly larger scale, improving smelting mills, building roads and employing more men. The industry was still expanding in the mid-nineteenth century, but the import of cheaper, foreign lead during the 1870s saw the start of its downfall, and the mines began to close.

Although leadmining has left its mark on Arkengarthdale, some of the best of the industry's buildings have disappeared, including the Great Octagon Mill, which stood half a mile to the north-west of the tiny village of Langthwaite. This smelting mill was built around 1700 by the Bathurst family, who owned the Manor of Arkengarthdale, to house a waterwheel and several furnaces. The mill was over 100 feet long, and its elongated octagonal form, centred on the thirty-six foot diameter waterwheel, was well-suited to give working space around the furnaces. But this fine building had decayed away to almost nothing by 1955. However, the nearby Old

Powder Magazine, a small, hexagonal stone structure built around 1804 to store gunpowder for the workings, still exists, standing alone in a meadow.

The church of St Mary the Virgin was erected in 1818 just to the north of Langthwaite, its relatively large size due to the influx of leadminers. It has a tall tower, while inside is a west gallery. It is the only example in the Dales of a commissioners' church, one of the 214 churches built by commissioners appointed under an act of parliament of 1818, which decreed that one million pounds of government funds should be spent on the construction of churches throughout the country.

Following the road up the dale (which became a turnpike in 1770) in three miles or so the old Toll House appears, a single-storey, two room cottage; one room was for official purposes, the other for the toll collector's family. The turnpike connected Reeth with Tan Hill, six miles to the west, where the Tan Hill Inn stands on the inhospitable moor. At a height of 1,732 feet above sea level, the inn is England's highest.

Head westward from Reeth to explore Swaledale. Most cottages in Healaugh date from the seventeenth or eighteenth centuries, though alterations have obscured many of their original features; north-west of the village, a bridlepath above Barney Beck leads to the remains of two lead-smelting mills. The walls of Surrender Smelt Mill, a couple of miles from the village, still stand high (it was built in 1839-41), while a mile further out, the Old Gang Smelt Mill complex is signalled by a tall chimney. The mill closed in 1898.

The main Swaledale road crosses the river at Gunnerside, and three miles west is Muker,

A typical Dales landscape: wall patterns in the fields of Swaledale. Many of these walls date from the eighteenth century.

where, apart from Swaledale vernacular cottages, may be found an Elizabethan church, St Mary. It was built in 1580 to serve the upper end of the dale. A mile or so west of Muker, the road divides, and Cliff Gate Road bears left to climb over Buttertubs Pass and enter Wensleydale.

Back on the main Swaledale road, the end of the dale is in sight at the pretty village of Keld, where a Methodist chapel emphasises the strong Nonconformist presence in nineteenth century Swaledale. The chapel was built in 1840-1 — there is a pleasing sundial dated 1840 — but rebuilt in 1860; inside, a gallery is supported by cast iron columns.

West of Keld there is only moorland and the watershed, marked by the unnatural assembly of tall cairns on Nine Standards Rigg, two miles to the north of the B6270 and six miles west of Keld (an often boggy walk

An unusual nave window, dating from restoration in 1683, on the south of the church of St Edmund King and Martyr at Marske.

Looking west up Swaledale towards Muker, from a bridlepath above Gunnerside. The church of St Mary stands on the highest point in Muker.

from the high point of the road). The clouds occasionally clear from the Nine Standards, which date at least from the eighteenth century, to reveal a tremendous view westward along the Pennine edge; eastward is the bleak moorland of upper Swaledale.

If the delights of Swaledale are exhausted, return to Richmond to explore its northern fringes and head towards Teesdale. On taking a northern exit from Richmond via Gilling Road, the B6274, in just under a mile the traveller is assailed by an excellently-sited

Oliver's Duckett, Richmond, with the Cleveland Hills in the distance. The folly takes its curious name from the surrounding area, which is known as Olliver, while Duckett probably stems from dovecot.

tower to the east. This is Oliver's Duckett, a battlemented, round tower, which is an eyecatcher for Aske Hall, standing nearly a mile to the west.

The hall originated as a medieval pele tower; further building by Thomas Wharton between 1611 and 1622 made it a substantial country house on an E-shaped plan, with a porch as the central arm. The hall and estate were purchased by London courtier Sir Conyers Darcy, a political enemy of the Whartons, in 1727, after the downfall of the previous owner caused by extravagance and political ineptitude.

Darcy improved the house, which had been much neglected, probably built Oliver's

Duckett, and erected a totally delightful Gothick garden building, the Temple, to the rear. His architects for the Temple were probably William Kent, who produced an initial drawing around 1735, and Daniel Garrett, who appears to have executed a rather different design about 1745. The main, octagonal tower of the Temple is flanked by two smaller turrets; the whole rises from an arcaded base and is decorated in the Gothick manner. It was probably used as a banqueting house.

In 1763, five years after Darcy's death, Aske was sold to the successful Scottish businessman Sir Lawrence Dundas, who already owned property at Marske-by-the-Sea, Upleatham and Loftus. John Carr made some improvements to the house around 1763-6, but his grand rebuilding scheme, dated 1767, was never put into practice, probably because Dundas was committed to work on his other properties, principally Moor Park in Hertfordshire. Dundas died in 1781, and his grandson was created Earl of Zetland in 1838. Dramatic alterations in the Classical style were made to Aske in 1961-3 under the direction of Claud Phillimore, continuing the evolution of the hall.

Turn left at the crossroads on the far side of Gilling West (look out for the Rock, a folly tower on a rocky outcrop in Sedbury Park to the east) and bear left after Hartforth, along a very narrow lane; in two miles, at a T-junction, left again and then right to find Kirby Hill, an inordinately pretty village, really little more than a quadrangle of buildings.

The church of St Peter and St Felix dates from the twelfth and fourteenth centuries, and has a particularly impressive tower, erected in 1397. The grammar school was built in 1556 as a combined school and almshouse, and funded by local cleric John Dakyn, whose monument resides in the church; it continued to function as a school until 1957. The old schoolroom has now become the village hall, while the master's lodging above is a Landmark Trust holiday flat.

The village of Ravensworth lies below and about a mile to the north of Kirby Hill. Here, there is a large and pleasant green, and the remains of Ravensworth Castle stand just to the south-east. The castle, stronghold of the Fitzhugh family, benefactors of Jervaulx Abbey, dates from at least the fourteenth century, but was abandoned in the sixteenth century; now its fragmentary ruins provide a romantic backdrop for the village. Much of the wall of the medieval deer park, south of the castle, still stands.

From Ravensworth or Kirby Hill, continue north-west along the edge of the moorland through the villages of Gayles, Dalton and Newsham to Barningham, where the road turns north to run alongside the River Greta and meet the horribly busy A66 at Greta Bridge. The bridge itself is a delicate, single-arched John Carr work of 1773, made famous in the watercolour by John Sell Cotman, painted in 1805. Just across the bridge (and well away from the main road) is the Morritt Arms, an atmospheric coaching inn with a surprise in the back bar; here, wall murals of Dickensian characters surround the drinker. They were painted in 1946 by J Gilroy, famed for his Guinness advertisements.

North-east of Greta Bridge, the byroad to Whorlton crosses the Tees on a delightful

Egglestone Abbey, a late twelfth century Premon-stratensian foundation, stands on the south bank of the River Tees just east of Barnard Castle. Here, the Tees forms the border between the North Riding and County Durham.

suspension bridge, built in 1829-31 by Newcastle-upon-Tyne architects John Green and his son Benjamin. The elder Green specialised in bridge construction, and the Whorlton example is the earliest in the country still supported by its original wrought iron chains.

South of Greta Bridge, a mile upstream and on the west bank of the Greta, are the ruins of old Brignall church, St Mary; either take the riverside footpath, or the road to Brignall and a short path east to the river. A new St Mary was built in the village in 1833-4.

Seven miles west along the River Greta is Bowes (access from the A66 or A67, four miles south-west of Barnard Castle). Bowes was the Roman settlement of Lavatrae, with a fort, aqueduct and bath-house. Within the bounds of the fort, Bowes Castle keep was built for Henry II in 1171-90, re-using some Roman materials. The keep, faced with beautifully-worked sandstone, stands three stories high. A Bowes school was the inadvertent model for the awful Dotheboys Hall in *Nicholas Nickleby*, published by Charles Dickens in 1838-9; Dickens himself stayed at the Unicorn Inn.

The gateway beside Greta Bridge reveals the presence of Rokeby Park, which stands just to the north, and was built by the extravagant amateur architect Sir Thomas Robinson in 1725-30. Robinson acquired his interest in architecture during his Grand Tour, and built Rokeby in the fashionable Palladian manner, adding original elements which make it a unique design. He also contrived a romantic setting for the house from the surrounding parkland. A path along the north side of the park leads over the Greta, almost at its meeting point with the Tees, to Mortham Tower, a mid-fourteenth century pele tower with later additions; the battlemented tower and archway are reminiscent of a toy fortress.

The Morritt Arms Hotel between the wars. The hotel, an old coaching inn, stands close to Greta Bridge, built by John Carr in 1773

A little over a mile north-west of Rokeby, the sublime remains of Egglestone Abbey stand beside a byroad, above the south bank of the Tees. The Premonstratensian abbey was founded between 1195 and 1198, and colonised from Easby Abbey, near Richmond (described in more detail on page 104). Egglestone was never a large community, although a sizeable church was built in the latter half of the thirteenth century. It suffered at the hands of Scots and English soldiers during the fourteenth century, and was dissolved in 1540; much of the abbey ended its days as building material. But the ruins, with several walls still standing to almost their full height, survive in a perfect rural setting.

The road from Egglestone leads north-west, following the Tees and giving fine views across the border to mighty Barnard Castle; just west of the bridge at Startforth, an aqueduct crosses the river, while three miles ahead is the village of Cotherstone, where a castle stood at the junction of the Tees with the River Balder.

At the north end of the village, just before the bridge, a byroad heads upstream along the Balder; in half a mile, look north for a nine-arch viaduct crossing the deep and narrow valley. Now redundant, it was built in 1868 by the Tees Valley Railway, which connected Barnard Castle with Middleton-in-Teesdale. Its stone arches are topped by a cast iron parapet.

Two miles further up Teesdale, along the B6277, takes us to Romaldkirk, a quietly pretty village laid out around a green. The church of St Romald, dating from the twelfth to fourteenth centuries, gave its name to the village; Romald is derived from Rumwald, the son of a king of Northumbria. The village as a whole is delightful, with a narrow passage leading out from the church to the large, irregular green, where cottages and more substantial houses are scattered.

Stay south of the Tees on a minor road, at the junction opposite Middleton-in-Teesdale, and head on to Holwick, where a track at the far end of the village will take the walker to the river and Wynch Bridge, close to Low Force waterfall.

The first bridge on the site was constructed around 1741, and was the first suspension bridge in Europe. It was used by leadminers from Holwick, who crossed the river to work in County Durham; an exciting journey, as the two foot wide bridge was provided with a handrail on only one side. A wider bridge was built around 1830, and in its turn this, too, was replaced.

Soon after Holwick the road peters out, but walkers can continue along by the Tees; High Force waterfall is less than a couple of miles upstream from Wynch Bridge, on an easy path shared with the Pennine Way.

For an idiosyncratic end to this tour of the northern dales, press on two miles from High Force to Cronkley Bridge, where the Pennine Way leaves us to cross the Tees. At the bridge, take the footpath which heads west along the south bank of the Tees, and in just over a mile, under the lee of Cronkley Scar, the river curves slightly north. Stand at the crown of the bend, and you will be the most northerly person, not just in the North Riding, but in the whole of Yorkshire.

DRUIDS IN A DALE OF FOLLIES

Wensleydale

LET US start our journey down Wensleydale, the valley of the River Ure, at
Hawes, where the gables and barge-
boards of the pretty Tudor railway station,
built in 1878, now look out over an abandoned
platform.

The Wensleydale line, between Hawes and
Northallerton, was run by the North Eastern
Railway, while the Midland Railway was
responsible for the six-mile westward link to
its Settle & Carlisle line at Garsdale Head, just
in the West Riding. Construction of this short
length of railway, over difficult moorland,
necessitated the building of several small
viaducts, the best of which stands near
Appersett; the village is a mile west of Hawes
on the A684. Turning off the main road, a little
way south along the road into Widdale, the
curving, five-arch Appersett Viaduct looms
large; it took the track across Widdale Beck,
and was designed by J S Crossley, who built
the whole of the Settle & Carlisle line.

Now, no trains run along Wensleydale. In
the upper dale, the line closed to passengers
in 1954, and the railway finally disappeared
from Hawes ten years later; Hawes Station is
now a National Park centre and museum. It
stands beside the road leading north of Hawes,
over Buttertubs Pass and into Swaledale. In
recent years, the line in the lower part of the
dale — east of Redmire, near Castle Bolton —
has been used solely for freight, carrying
limestone from the quarries at Redmire to
Teesside, but this service finally ceased in
early 1993.

Hawes itself is a busy market town; it was
granted a market charter in 1700, and was also
something of a textile centre, but poor
communications eventually put an end to this
industry.

Ropemaking, once as ubiquitous as
brewing, did prosper in Hawes, and the
ropeworks stands at Town Foot, a little way
from the station on the main road. The
ropeworks moved to its present site in 1921.

To the west, near the market place, is the
church of St Margaret of Antioch, built in 1851
to replace a medieval chapel. Its elegant

furniture was designed around 1930 by the woodcarver Thompson of Kilburn.

Head south of the market place and out of town on to the fields, where a stone-flagged path, a friendly half-mile section of the Pennine Way, takes the walker to the hamlet of Gayle. Here are substantial remains of the textile industry: a water-powered mill, built around 1784, stands above Gayle Beck; and a late eighteenth century wool warehouse is nearby. The mill first produced cotton, then woollen yarn, but became a saw-mill in the late nineteenth century.

Four miles down the dale from Hawes is Bainbridge, either via the main A684 or preferably the quieter byroad on the north bank of the Ure, which crosses the river at Yore Bridge, rebuilt by John Carr in 1793, to reach the village.

Bainbridge has a fine green, overlooked on its north side by the Rose and Crown Hotel, whose interior has seventeenth century panelling and a grape-strewn frieze dating from a century before. The village lacks a church but was well-provided with alternative places of worship: a Methodist chapel (1836); a Congregational chapel in Italianate style, built in 1864 and now converted to housing; and a nineteenth century Friends Meeting House. A charming Temperance Hall, in a local interpretation of Arts and Crafts style, was built in 1910 at the south-western edge of the village.

The earthworks of Virosidum — the largest Roman fort in the Dales — still stand guard east of Bainbridge on Brough Hill, which looks out over Raydale, the valley of the River Bain. Footpaths and byroads lead south-west along the valley from either side of the Bain Bridge, at the southern end of Bainbridge green, near a series of waterfalls.

Two miles up the dale at Countersett, just north of Semerwater, a natural lake, is an intriguing collection of buildings, including the old Boar Inn of 1667 and Countersett Hall (1652), where early Quaker meetings were held before the building of the nearby Meeting House in 1710.

Half a mile south-west of the lake, the path along the southern side of Raydale passes an isolated graveyard — still in use — beside a deserted and ruined chapel dating from 1722, before heading uphill to the tiny hamlet of Stalling Busk and the church of St Matthew, which superseded the chapel. It was built in 1908-9 by Gerard Davidson, and brings to mind a Swiss chalet, with its steeply-pitched roof and protruding bellcote.

North of Bainbridge, the Wensleydale byroad crosses the river and turns east for Askrigg, but look out for the excellent Coleby Hall, an E-shaped mansion built in 1655, on the hillside just north of Yore Bridge. On the roadside is the Primitive Methodist chapel, dating from 1858 but rebuilt, with a surprisingly flashy façade, in 1908.

At the western end of Askrigg stands the largest church in Wensleydale, St Oswald; it originated as a chapel of ease around 1175, but much was added in the fifteenth and sixteenth centuries. The interior is a little disappointing. The windows are mainly clear glass, which allows light to flood in and overwhelm any decorative subtleties.

The prosperity of Askrigg was due to its market, granted in 1587 (the market cross is a replacement of 1830-1) and its position on two turnpikes; substantial Georgian buildings, in particular the Kings Arms Hotel, make a pleasing townscape.

At the east end of Askrigg, the road forks: only a mile east, along the Wensleydale byroad, is twin-towered Nappa Hall, a fortified manor house built in 1459; but rather than this deviation, head south to cross the Ure on a narrow bridge and meet the A684 at Worton. Between the bridge and the main road stands Worton Hall, a farmhouse built in 1600, which has several fine, mullioned windows.

At Aysgarth, seven miles down the dale, is the church of St Andrew. It stands about half a mile east of the village, beside the road which leads off the A684 and down to Aysgarth Falls. St Andrew existed as early as Norman times, and was originally the parish church for the whole of upper Wensleydale; it was almost completely rebuilt in 1865-6. Inside the church is a wonderful carved rood screen, which was removed from Jervaulx Abbey after its dissolution. The colourful screen dominates the chancel, which also contains the vicar's stall, made from a pair of beautifully-carved bench ends, once part of the abbot's stall at Jervaulx. Screen and stall were both the work of the Ripon school of carvers, and date from around 1506.

Continue over the Ure and east through Carperby to Castle Bolton, where the hugely impressive remains of Bolton Castle sit high above the dale. It was built between 1378 and 1399 for Sir Richard Scrope, Lord High Chancellor, by the master-mason John Lewyn; fear of Scots invasion meant defence was paramount, but comfort was also important, and the four-towered, rectangular, courtyard castle was designed to be a palatial home. Private rather than communal accommodation,

for individuals and some households, was a great innovation at Bolton, and was a precursor of later country-house design. The castle eventually made an ideal prison, secure yet comfortable, for Mary, Queen of Scots, who was imprisoned at Bolton during 1568-9.

The church of St Oswald, next to the castle, was built about 1325, and stands at the head of the village street; Castle Bolton is a planned village, and the twin rows of cottages flanking its long green make a perfect setting for the castle.

But to find some follies — an antidote to this formality — return to the main road by way of the bridge at Aysgarth, turn briefly east along the A684, then head south for West Burton, at the foot of pretty, secluded Bishopdale. There is a fine obelisk on the village green, which is surrounded by as good a collection of buildings as any in Wensleydale, but follow the B6160 north for a glimpse of the West Burton follies, not an end-of-the-pier show but a weird set of structures at Sorrelsykes Park.

Sorrelsykes, an early nineteenth century house with additions of 1921, stands east of the road, and beyond, on a meadow terrace, is a line of three small but unusual follies, which can be more closely inspected by taking the footpath (to Flanders Hall) from Edgley Farm. The most southerly, built around 1921, resembles a large pepperpot, then comes a low gateway, and finally a tall, conical affair, known locally as the Rocket Ship. The latter dates from about 1860. The threesome appear to be eyecatchers for Sorrelsykes, whose various owners, perhaps, designed the follies.

Back on the main road and continuing down the dale, look out for a more formal

*The Rocket Ship, built around
1860, and a pepperpot-shaped
fellow folly at Sorrelsykes Park,
near West Burton.*

folly to the north as the land rises, just before Swinithwaite. This octagonal, domed, Classical tower, hiding in the undergrowth opposite Temple Farm, was once part of the pleasure garden of Swinithwaite Hall, which stands almost a mile away on the eastern edge of the village. The tower was designed by John Foss of Richmond in 1792; he was trained as a mason by his stepfather, then taught himself architecture and specialised in country houses. He also became Mayor of Richmond. The name Temple Farm arises from the presence of the Knights Templars, who built a chapel on the bank to the south-east of the farm around 1200; its remains are still visible.

A mile further, at West Witton, take the road which climbs steeply south out of Wensleydale and drops down into isolated Coverdale at Melmerby; two miles east is Coverham, not so much a hamlet as a lonely church, with the ruins of an abbey nearby. But the dale was not always so quiet; coal and lead mines were worked here in medieval times, and stone was quarried, so that when the Premonstratensians settled in Coverham in 1212, the area would have been fairly prosperous. Part of the thirteenth century west wall of Coverham Abbey survives, as well as sections of the fourteenth century arcade, rebuilt after damaging Scottish raids.

Holy Trinity Church was built in the thirteenth century, and was probably served by canons from the abbey; many later additions resulted in a substantial church with a beautiful setting, but its most memorable features date from the restoration which took place in 1878. These are the brightly-coloured glazed tiles which cover the east walls of the chancel and south aisle. They were probably

This folly near Swinithwaite, a decorative octagonal tower built in 1792, was once part of the pleasure garden of Swinithwaite Hall.

produced by Maw & Co of Jackfield in Shropshire, one of the leading nineteenth century tilemakers. Initially the shining, multicoloured surface — there is much green, pink and purple — is disconcerting, giving an overly institutional impression, but this now-redundant building is a peaceful spot for contemplation, and soon the tiles begin to seem perfectly apt.

From Coverham, go west and back into Wensleydale via Agglethorpe, dropping down to cross the Ure at Wensley, the village which gave its name to the dale. The attractive stone bollards on Wensley Bridge were added during widening in 1818.

Wensley held a market from 1289, but a visit from the plague in 1563 left the village deserted, and the neglected church tower blew down in 1709. Now, however, Holy Trinity has a fully-restored tower, rebuilt in 1719, to set off the largely thirteenth century nave and chancel (the aisles date from the fourteenth century). Inside is fine sixteenth century

Holy Trinity Church, Coverham, built in the thirteenth century but much altered. The tower dates from the sixteenth and seventeenth centuries. In the churchyard are some fine gravestones, several with the inscription on a brass plate, as was the local custom.

woodwork produced by the well-known Ripon school of carvers.

Just north of Wensley Bridge is the east lodge and gateway of Bolton Hall, which lies a mile back up the dale, but can easily be seen across the valley from the main road. The first hall was erected in 1678 for the first Duke of Bolton, but the brick-built hall we see today is the result of complete reconstruction following a fire in 1902. The replacement is similar in appearance to the original, with a U-shaped main block and a lower wing to each side, all designed in a basic Georgian manner with prominent sash windows.

The thriving and enjoyable market town of Leyburn is only a mile or two down the dale from Wensley; it grew in importance as Wensley declined, and gained its market in 1584. The large, rectangular market place is dominated by the old town hall, a Classical pile erected by the lord of the manor, Lord Bolton, in 1856.

East of Leyburn the A684 leaves the Ure and runs east towards Bedale, soon passing through Constable Burton. To the north of the road lies Burton Park and Constable Burton Hall, a petite Palladian villa designed by John Carr and built for Sir Marmaduke Asty Wyvill in 1762-7; the Wyvill family owned the estate from the fifteenth century. This little Georgian showpiece, with its splendid Ionic recessed portico, replaced a Robert Smythson-style Elizabethan mansion (which Carr seems to have demolished in error).

Stay close to the Ure by taking the A6108 south from Leyburn, which crosses the river in a mile, through the arches of the unexpectedly martial Middleham Bridge. The original bridge of 1829-30 was an early

The castellated silhouette of Middleham Bridge, built in 1829-30 to cross the River Ure midway between Middleham and Leyburn.

suspension design, combining relatively new and untested technology with the Gothic style, used for the pairs of battlemented towers from which the wrought iron cables were hung at either end of the deck. The architects were Joseph Hansom, inventor of the Hansom cab and founder of the prestigious trade magazine *The Builder*, and Edward Welch, then in partnership at York. The bridge failed

The tiled reredos of Holy Trinity Church, Coverham. The tiles, probably manufactured by Maw & Co, were installed during the restoration of 1878.

quite soon after opening, probably due to vibrations caused by a herd of cattle being driven across, and its eventual replacement in 1865 consisted of vertical columns supporting simple cast iron beams, which carried the roadway.

Middleham stands a mile to the south-east of its bridge, and is a picturesque marriage of castle and church with working town; racehorses have been trained here since the eighteenth century. The earliest signs of settlement are eleventh century earthworks

Looking out over Wensleydale from the twelfth century keep of Middleham Castle.

just south-west of the castle on Williams Hill; these fortifications were constructed by Ribald, who was granted Middleham by his brother Alan the Red, builder of Richmond Castle, in 1086. The massive keep of the present castle was built in the 1170s, while the surrounding curtain walls largely date from the thirteenth century. The keep stands almost to its full height and gives fine views over town and dale.

In 1270, through marriage, the castle became the property of the Neville family of County Durham; it was home to Richard of Gloucester (brother of Edward IV) from 1461 when Richard Neville, Earl of Warwick, was Lord of Middleham. Warwick, a great power-broker who was known as the Kingmaker, failed in his rebellion against Edward and was killed at the Battle of Barnet in 1471. Richard of Gloucester married Warwick's daughter Anne in 1472, and was allowed by the king to take over Middleham, where their son Edward was born the following year. But in 1483 Richard seized the throne to become King

Richard III, setting off the third phase of the Wars of the Roses. The mysterious death of young Edward at Middleham in 1484 was then followed by the death of his father at the Battle of Bosworth Field in 1485. After Richard's death, Middleham Castle declined in importance, but the monumental walls — ten to twelve feet thick — of the keep's twin chambers are still solidly impressive.

The church of St Mary and St Alkelda is north of the castle, across Swine Market and down a lane leading into the churchyard. Although a plan of the church exists dating from 1280, the earliest surviving parts of the present building result from enlargements made in 1340.

Richard III, a keen religious benefactor, founded a college based on Middleham Church in 1477; collegiate status entitled the church and townspeople to a great degree of independence from the ecclesiastical authorities. These privileges continued even after Richard's death, and only in the eighteenth century was the arrangement of pews within the church altered to reflect the college's decline: box pews (since removed) replaced the college chapel-style seating. An Act of Parliament in 1845 finally ended the right of Middleham to be a royal peculiar, which ran its own affairs, and the church became a normal parish church.

The houses and hotels around elongated, sloping Market Place reflect the prosperity of Georgian Middleham, while to the west in Swine Market the heavyweight Baroque drinking fountain, erected in 1887 to mark the jubilee of Queen Victoria, is overlooked by the odd tower of the Gothic national school (1869), now an arts centre. Next door but one, Sundial

The sundial, dated 1778, on Sundial House, Middleham; the maker's name is towards the top, above the style (the indicator which casts a shadow on the face of the sundial).

House displays a good sundial of 1778, complete with the maker's name, Gargrave.

Head east along the A6108 from Middleham for just over a mile, then turn off to the left immediately before Cover Bridge, and cross the Ure at hefty, stone Ulshaw Bridge, built in 1673-4. On the right is the Roman Catholic church of St Simon and St Jude, surprisingly attached to the rear of what appears to be a Georgian house, in fact the presbytery, which dates from 1695.

The delightful little church, with its cone-topped octagonal tower, owes its presence to the Scrope family of Danby Hall, a mile to the east. The Scropes were staunch Catholics, and several of their number were buried in the church crypt during the eighteenth and

The church of St Simon and St Jude, Ulshaw Bridge, was rebuilt in 1868 by Joseph Hansom for the Scrope family of nearby Danby Hall.

nineteenth centuries. St Simon and St Jude was rebuilt in 1868 by Simon Thomas Scrope. His architect was also a Catholic, Joseph Hansom, who had worked for Scrope at Danby Hall in 1855. The hall was based around a fourteenth century pele tower or fortified house, with much later building, to which Hansom added the south front and terrace.

Back over Ulshaw Bridge and across Cover Bridge lies the early nineteenth century planned village of East Witton, laid out around a long green running from east to west off the main road.

The village owes its existence to the Earl of Ailesbury, whose ancestors had been in possession of the estate since 1603. He built

Jervaulx Park, where the ruins of Jervaulx Abbey stand in an idyllic setting close to the River Ure.

the oversized church of St John the Evangelist at the eastern end of the village in 1809-12, to commemorate the fiftieth anniversary of the accession of George III to the throne. The earl chose as his architect Henry Hake Seward, a pupil of Sir John Soane, who had just gone into practice on his own account. Seward's large and expensive Gothic church, built of sandstone, would look more at home in an urban environment; alterations in 1872 included the addition of the Perpendicular east window.

The original settlement lay to the south-east of the present East Witton, on the lane leading south from the sharp bend in the main road. The old village is said to have been burnt out, and its small church, St Martin, was demolished when the new St John was erected; the peaceful churchyard, however, survives. The earl's estate village consists of a school built in 1817 (now a house), and two rows of stone cottages.

The narrow lane running west between the cottages leads into Coverdale, passing Braithwaite Hall in a couple of miles. This imposing manor house, built in 1667, stands on the hillside to the south of the road. There are tall chimneys, mullioned windows, and on the north façade are three large gables, each with an oval, blind window.

Two miles east of East Witton, at a another sharp bend on the A6108, look out for a gateway topped by three plump ball-finials. It was erected in 1864 and fronts nineteenth century Jervaulx Hall; hidden behind the hall, in the rampant greenery of Jervaulx Park and close to the Ure, are the romantic ruins of Jervaulx Abbey. This is not a well-regimented, neat and tidy remnant from the past, but a

The ruins of Jervaulx Abbey, built by the Cistercians in the twelfth century.

serene, ivy-clad, most picturesque and evoc-ative collection of stones. Sheep and cattle happily graze all around. Although little remains above ground of the 264 foot long abbey church, the south wall of the monks' dormitory stands high, and much more; the six octagonal columns which supported the vaults of the chapter house are particularly fine.

Jervaulx Abbey: the remains of the octagonal columns which supported the vaults of the chapter house, just east of the cloister.

The Cistercian foundation settled at Jervaulx in 1156, immediately began building, and continued construction into the second half of the twelfth century; most of the visible remains date from this period. The last abbot of Jervaulx was wrongly accused of taking part in the northern rebellion of 1536, the Pilgrimage of Grace; he was imprisoned in the Tower of London and executed at Tyburn. In an act of revenge on the part of the Crown, the remaining monks were expelled from the abbey and the buildings blown up. Apart from its ruinous state, there is now no hint of a violent past at Jervaulx, one of the most peaceful historic sites in the North Riding.

Five miles south-east is Masham, where the impressive Black Sheep Brewery looks out across the Ure, and the prominent spire of St Mary's Church forms a backdrop to activities in spacious Market Place. There was

The church of St Mary at Masham. Its spire dates from the fifteenth century, although it was restored after being damaged by lightning in 1855.

The Druids' Temple, built by William Danby of Swinton Park, near Masham, in the early nineteenth century. The construction of this functional folly provided employment for local labourers, while showing Danby — something of an eccentric — to be aware of the contemporary fashion for the Druid cult.

a church here in Saxon times (part of an early ninth century cross stands in the churchyard, near the porch), but the tower was built in the twelfth and thirteenth centuries, while the spire was added in the fifteenth century. The bulk of the church was rebuilt in the fourteenth and fifteenth centuries. The interior, much restored in the nineteenth century, holds memorials to leading local landowners, including members of the Danby and Cunliffe Lister families, successive owners of the nearby Swinton estate. Bradford textile magnate Samuel Cunliffe Lister, later Lord Masham, also bought the Jervaulx estate in 1887.

Masham Church was given to York Minster in the mid-twelfth century by the Lord of

Mashamshire; it became a canonry, and its high revenues led to it becoming known as the Golden Prebend of York. An assortment of high-flying clerics were associated with Masham as canons, although more mundane vicars actually served local needs. The link with York was severed by Henry VIII in 1545, when he gave the patronage of the living to Trinity College, Cambridge, where it has remained to this day.

Masham lies at the foot of Colsterdale, the pretty but little-known valley of the River Burn; the byroad from Masham runs along its northern edge, through Fearby to Healey and the church of St Paul, built in 1848 by Edward Buckton Lamb, renowned for his picturesque approach to church architecture. The interior of St Paul, with its inordinately narrow tower, is no disappointment.

A little before Healey the road plunges steeply into the dale, crosses the Burn and, turning east, eventually emerges at the fine east gates of Swinton Park, a castellated mansion built by its owner, William Danby (1752-1833), over a period of about fifty years up to the 1820s.

The original early eighteenth century house was altered by John Carr in 1764-7, then Danby, a keen if eccentric builder, set about the task of reconstruction. He was assisted by a fine array of architectural talent: John Foss of Richmond built the north range in 1791-6 and the south wing in 1813-14; Gothic designer James Wyatt was called in to decorate the drawing room around 1793-4; and Robert Lugar, a London architect who specialised in the Picturesque, remodelled the entire edifice in 1821-4, adding the great round tower and the castellations.

It is a splendid building, but it did not completely fulfil its owner's urge to build. Danby was a benevolent landlord, and combined his love of architecture with alleviating local unemployment in a most unusual project: the construction of his very own version of Stonehenge. To see the Druids' Temple, follow the road south and west around Swinton Park, heading for Ilton; a mile north of this little hamlet, turn west for almost a further mile down a Forestry Commission track to a car park, then take the footpath into the wood.

In a cool clearing is an oval of grey standing stones, linked by cross-stones, all surrounding an altar, with occasional solitary stones set nearby in the woodland. It is totally convincing, and a wonderful testament to the power of fashion, for the Druid cult was much in vogue during the early nineteenth century. The thoughts of the labourers, earning a shilling a day for their work, are not recorded.

But this most workmanlike folly, an architectural daydream and perhaps the builders' delight, makes a fitting end to a journey through the North Riding.

Glossary of Architectural Terms

apse Semicircular end to a building, normally a chancel or chapel.

arboretum A collection of trees, often of unusual species.

arcade Series of arches supported by columns; may be free-standing or attached to a building. Also means a covered way lined with shops.

Art Deco Popular interwar style which took the place of Art Nouveau *(qv)*; characterised by geometric forms and bold colour. Its name originated from a 1925 Paris exhibition of decorative arts.

Art Nouveau Style at its height around 1900, which appeared in the mid-1880s and lasted until the first decade of the twentieth century. Its hallmarks were flowing, organic forms and curving lines.

Arts and Crafts Late Victorian movement emphasising craft skills, exemplified by the work of William Morris & Co. Its decorative motifs were often derived from natural objects, while in architecture it featured new uses of vernacular *(qv)* forms.

ashlar Blocks of stone cut with square edges, finished smoothly and laid in even courses.

attached column Column which is not completely free-standing, but linked with a wall to the rear.

bailey Open area of a castle.

ball finial Finial *(qv)* in the shape of a globe.

bargeboard A protective wooden plank attached to the inclined gable *(qv)* ends of a building, often carved decoratively. '

Baroque Late seventeenth and early eighteenth century architectural style, using massive, complex, curving forms in bold fashion.

barrel vault Vault *(qv)* with a semicircular cross-section.

bastion A projection at the corner of a fortification, often a turret or tower.

battered Wall with an inclined slope.

battlements The alternately raised and lowered upper edge of a parapet wall, often a castle wall.

bay Vertical segment of a building defined by its fenestration *(qv)*.

beakhead Norman *(qv)* decorative motif resembling a row of bird heads with projecting beaks.

belvedere Summer-house with a view, often sited on a hill in a park. Also a viewing tower or turret on top of a house.

bow Curved, and usually mainly glazed, projection from the wall of a building.

box pew Georgian *(qv)* church bench enclosed by high, wooden panels and having a small door.

breastshot Waterwheel in which water is fed on to the wheel at its vertical mid-point.

Bronze Age   British era following the Stone Age and lasting from around 2100 BC to 700 BC. It was marked by the use of bronze for tools, and the construction of stone circles.

buttress   Massive element of brickwork or stonework projecting from a wall and supporting the structure.

canted   An oblique corner, often used of bay windows with a non-rectangular section.

campanile   Bell tower separate from its parent building; also used to describe isolated chimneys.

capital head   The uppermost part of a column, often decorated.

castellated   Having turrets and battlements (*qv*), as in a castle.

chancel   Area forming the east end of a church; the main altar is placed in the chancel, which is reserved for clergy and choir.

chancel arch   Church archway at the west end of the chancel, normally dividing the nave from the chancel.

chantry chapel   Chapel endowed to celebrate masses as ordered by its founder.

chapel of ease   Chapel built to enable members of a congregation living distant from the parish church to attend serices locally.

chapter house   Part of the eastern range (*qv*) of monastic buildings next to the cloister (a covered arcade), often circular or polygonal in plan. It was used by the monks for discussion of all types of monastic business.

charterhouse   Community of the Carthusian monastic order consisting of a collection of individual cells.

choir   In a church, the section of the chancel where service is sung.

Classical   Various forms of Classical style dominated English architecture from the early seventeenth century until the early nineteenth century. It was originally inspired by Greek and Roman architecture, and then by Renaissance interpretations of past styles. Classical buildings featured traditionally correct proportions and severely-restrained decoration.

clerestory   Uppermost part of the main walls of a building, with a series of windows; a term often used in church architecture to describe a nave with windows in the upper storey.

cockpit   A pit, often circular in cross-section, where game-cocks fought.

colonnade   Linked series of columns.

Corinthian   Order of Classical (*qv*) architecture involving specified proportions of column and capital, with elaborate foliage decoration of the latter.

crenellate   Crenellations are also known as battlements (*qv*); a crenellated wall has alternating higher and lower sections along its upper edge.

crocket   Decorative element, often carved in leaf shapes, which appears on Gothic (*qv*) spires, gables (*qv*) and other pre-eminent features.

crossing tower   Church tower sited above the area where nave, chancel and transepts intersect.

curtain wall   Originally the outer wall of a castle, connecting its towers, but now also applied to any external non-load-bearing wall.

dado   Decorative finish of the lower part (to about waist height) of an internal wall.

Decorated   See Gothic.

Doric   Order of Classical (*qv*) architecture involving specified proportions of column and capital, with very little decoration of the latter.

dovecot   Structure in which pigeons were kept for breeding.

Early English   See Gothic.

Edwardian   Building design in the first decade of the twentieth century encompassed a range of styles, from severe Classical to highly-decorative Edwardian Baroque. These may perhaps all be characterised by a preoccupation with novel interpretations of existing styles, and the search for a new and British architecture. The resulting buildings differed widely in appearance but shared a certain confidence.

Egyptian Revival   The use of motifs, such as obelisks (*qv*) and pyramids, derived from ancient Egyptian architecture. The early nineteenth century and the 1920s are the two most recent revivals, the latter resulting from the discovery in 1922 of the tomb of Tutankhamun.

Elizabethan   Style of late sixteenth and early seventeenth centuries typified by symmetrical façades, large, mullioned (*qv*) and transomed (*qv*) windows, and decorative strapwork (*qv*).

encaustic tile   Clay tile of the Victorian period, used mainly as flooring, with decoration originally based on Medieval tile designs. Later Victorian examples featured colourful geometric decoration, and were widely used in public buildings as well as churches.

eyecatcher   Building, normally in a park or garden, erected to enhance the view.

faience   Inclusive term for all ceramic materials used in an architectural context, such as on a faience façade.

fenestration   The pattern of windows in the wall of a building.

finial   Decorative feature of varying form found on the top of spires, gables (*qv*) and other tall architectural elements; originally Gothic (*qv*).

flying buttress   Buttress (*qv*) with its lower part detached from the building it supports.

folly   Building with no purpose, at least in terms of normal cost-benefit criteria. Follies are often decorative, with eccentric architectural features, and frequently appear as park ornaments.

gable   The triangular upper part of a wall defined by a pitched roof. Variants include the Dutch gable, which has curved sides and is topped by a pediment (*qv*).

Georgian   Architectural style of the early eighteenth to early nineteenth centuries, with plain, Classical (*qv*) exteriors and more decorative interiors, culminating in those of Robert Adam in the late eighteenth century.

Germano-Gothic   Victorian style in which Gothic (*qv*) is tempered by traditional German elements, particularly turrets, gables and steeply-pitched roofs with small dormer windows.

Gothic   Style featuring pointed arches, arcading (*qv*) and flying buttresses (*qv*); together they formed a structural system which minimised wall area. It was introduced to Britain in the early twelfth century, becoming known by the late twelfth century as the Early English style. This developed into the Decorated style, with more prominent decoration and tracery (*qv*), in the late thirteenth century. By the second half of the fourteenth century the Perpendicular style, with the emphasis on straight, vertical elements, had come to the fore and lasted for around 250 years. The Victorian Gothic Revival was particularly important for church architecture.

Gothick   Style of the Gothic *(qv)* Revival of the mid-eighteenth century, which was first applied to pleasure buildings and featured frilly, highly-decorative Gothic motifs.

hammerbeam roof   Roof structure formed by series of roof supports or hammer-posts projecting vertically upward from brackets or hammerbeams set in the top of the wall.

High Victorian   Architecture of the mid-nineteenth century, often featuring poly-chromy *(qv)* and the use of varied building materials.

ice-house   Garden outbuilding popular in eighteenth and nineteenth centuries, often built with country houses; its purpose was to store ice. Frequently built partly underground, and with a roughly egg-shaped internal space.

Ionic   Order of Classical *(qv)* architecture involving specified proportions of column and capital, with twin spiral-pattern decoration of the latter.

Iron Age   Period from around 700 BC until the time of the Roman invasion; iron was used for tools and weapons.

Italianate   Victorian style involving Italian Renaissance elements such as low-pitched roofs, towers and round-headed windows.

Jacobean   Style of the early seventeenth century, a development of the Elizabethan *(qv)*; important elements were large windows, extravagant decoration and dominant gables *(qv)*.

Jacobethan   Victorian or Edwardian style combining elements traditionally found in Jacobean *(qv)* and Elizabethan *(qv)* buildings, such as mullioned *(qv)* windows, a high level of decoration and prominent gables *(qv)*.

king post   Central, vertical timber supporting a pitched roof, and rising from a beam connecting the tops of the walls to the ridge of the roof.

lancet window   Narrow, pointed-arched window.

lychgate   Covered gateway at the entrance to a churchyard; it originally provided a resting place for a coffin.

mansard roof   Pitched roof with two differently sloping sections on each side: a steeper section rising from the wall followed by a lower-pitched section reaching the ridge.

medieval   The era between the fifth and fifteenth centuries, from when the Romans left Britain to the coming of the Renaissance. In architectural terms, it encompasses Saxon *(qv)*, Norman *(qv)*, Romanesque *(qv)* and Gothic *(qv)* periods.

menagerie   A collection of wild animals, usually exhibited in cages.

misericord   Bracket, often decoratively carved, on the underside of a hinged choir stall or seat; when the stall was raised, the misericord supported the standing chorister.

Moorish   Stylistic features used in the late Victorian period and taken from the ancient Islamic architecture of Spain and North Africa; its main forms are elaborate domes and arcades.

motte   A piled-up mound of earth and rubble, which was a common Norman *(qv)* defensive structure.

mullion   Vertical element separating the sections of a window.

nave   Area forming the west end of a church, which may be extended to the north or south with aisles.

Norman   Architecture of the period from the early eleventh to the mid-twelfth centuries. Its main features are massive structures, round-headed arches and geometrical ornament.

obelisk Tall, upright column, usually with a square cross-section and tapering towards the top.

openwork Describes a structure, often decorative, comprising interconnected building members; the network forms a pattern with spaces between the members. It may be a hollow structure, or take two-dimensional form.

oriel Bay window on an upper floor, which is unsupported at ground level, and thus overhanging.

overshot Waterwheel in which the water arrives at the top of the wheel, turning the wheel in the direction of the water flow.

Palladian Classical *(qv)* style derived from the buildings of the sixteenth century Italian architect Andrea Palladio, which was introduced to England in the early seventeenth century. The style emphasises symmetry and ancient systems of proportion, and strongly features the colonnade *(qv)*, portico *(qv)* and venetian window *(qv)*.

pantile Roof tile of S-shaped cross-section introduced into Britain from Holland in the seventeenth century, then manufactured in Britain from the start of the eighteenth century.

pediment Low-pitched gable *(qv)* above features such as a portico *(qv)*, door or window.

Perpendicular Gothic *(qv)* style dominant between the late fourteenth century and the late sixteenth century, when the Elizabethan *(qv)* style became established. Perpendicular style strongly emphasised vertical architectural elements, as did the more decorative Elizabethan.

Picturesque Mid-eighteenth to early nineteenth century style, largely used in the context of cottages, country houses and garden design but having broader implications, and partly derived from the images of seventeenth century landscape painting. The style was highly decorative, combining ruggedness with ruins, and used disparate elements such as Italianate *(qv)* motifs in an asymmetrical fashion. The object was to create a sublime vision by combining nature and architecture.

pilaster Column projecting only slightly from a wall.

pitchback Waterwheel in which the water arrives at the top of the wheel, turning the wheel in the opposite direction to the water flow.

polychromy Decorated in many colours. Mid-Victorian architects produced polychromy not only by using paint, but by combining different building materials; this technique is known as structural polychromy.

porte cochere A porch providing sufficient covered area for a carriage or other wheeled vehicle to pass beneath; sometimes found at railway stations or country houses.

portico Entrance space of a building, often a house or church, which is covered but normally open to the sides, and has a pediment *(qv)* supported by columns; the whole is in the style of a temple.

prodigy house Large-scale Elizabethan *(qv)* country house, with huge areas of glazing and abundant decoration.

Queen Anne Revival The architectural style used for small domestic buildings of the Queen Anne period (early eighteenth century) was revived in the late nineteenth century; in its revival form it emphasised red-brick walls and contrasting white, wooden window frames.

range   A row of buildings.

Regency   Style predominant between the 1790s and the early 1840s; when used strictly, the term relates to the period 1811-20 when the future George IV was prince regent. This neo-Classical style made free use of ancient forms, resulting in eclectic versions of Classical (*qv*) structures, which sometimes verged on the Picturesque (*qv*).

reredos   Screen or similar structure sited behind, and usually above, the altar; often decorated.

Rococo   The final stylistic phase of the Baroque (*qv*), which occurred during the mid-eighteenth century in England, where it was used only for interiors and garden buildings. The elaborately decorative Rococo style emphasised delicacy and lightness of form and colour, as opposed to the sombre heaviness of the Baroque.

Roman   Buildings of the Roman occupation of Britain, which lasted from around AD 43 to AD 409, and included sophisticated baths and temples.

Romanesque   Term used to describe the dominant architectural style of Europe from the tenth century (or before) until the eleventh century, and marked by the use of the round arch; roughly equivalent to the Norman (*qv*) style in Britain. The round-arched Romanesque form also underwent a late Victorian revival.

rood loft   The wooden rood or cross was usually erected at the east end of the nave, on a beam stretching across the upper part of the chancel arch (*qv*). Just below it was the rood loft, a gallery which might itself carry the rood or other images; the loft also stretched across the chancel arch. Rood lofts were introduced in the fifteenth century.

rood screen   Screen beneath the rood loft (*qv*), separating the nave and chancel.

rose window   Large, circular, church window, with its tracery (*qv*) pattern radiating from the centre.

rubblestone   Unfinished stone in various shapes, with rough surfaces and few right-angled corners; irregular rubble may be worked into horizontal courses during building, in which case it is known as coursed rubblestone.

rustication   Massive blocks of masonry which are separated by deep, V-shaped joints; often used on the lower part of external walls of large buildings to add weight to the overall composition.

Saxon   English architecture of the seventh to early eleventh centuries. Simple churches occurred in the seventh century, and towers first appeared in the tenth century; basic geometric decoration was often prominent.

Scottish Baronial   Style originated by architect William Burn around 1830 for Scottish country houses, in which the basic building was adorned with large, circular towers and turrets, often capped by steeply-pitched, conical roofs; the whole was in the Scottish tradition of fortified architecture.

Second Empire   Style current from the 1850s until the end of the nineteenth century; the main elements emphasised the height of the building: turrets, chimneys, domes and the mansard roof (*qv*). The term arises from extensions to the Louvre made by Napoleon III, which used French Renaissance decorative forms.

solar   Upper living-room of a medieval house.

spandrel   Roughly triangular area between

the tops of adjacent arches or arched windows; may be decorated.

staithe A jetty projecting from a land base above an area of water, along which wagons ran to empty their loads into ships below. Staithe may also refer to a wharf.

strapwork Late sixteenth century decorative motif of intertwined bands.

tie beam Main horizontal beam in a roof structure, which connects the tops of opposing walls.

timber-framed Type of building construction in which an open, wooden framework, usually consisting of horizontal and vertical timbers, forms the walls; this frame is then filled in with non-structural matter such as plaster.

tower house A medieval fortified house, of three storeys or more in height, most frequently found in Scotland and the north of England.

tracery Pattern of ribs defining the glazing of the upper section of a window; also used to describe the pattern of decoration on vaults (qv).

transom Horizontal element separating the sections of a window.

Tudor Architecture of the sixteenth century, culminating in the Elizabethan (qv) period, when the professional architect came to prominence for the first time.

tympanum The space between the top of the frame of a door, and the arch above; often semi-circular in shape.

undershot Waterwheel in which the water passes along the lower edge of the wheel.

vault Arched roof structure, normally in brick or stone, with a semicircular or more complex cross-section; a more complex vault is divided by a pattern of curved ribs.

venetian window Window in three vertical sections, of which the central section is taller than the side sections and has a semicircular top.

vermiculated Type of rustication (qv) in which the blocks of masonry are carved with intersecting, curving shapes having the appearance of worm tracks.

vernacular The architecture of everyday buildings, with the emphasis on the use of locally-available materials, as opposed to the style of grander buildings designed by architects.

vestry Small room, in which the vestments are kept, attached to a church.

Victorian Architecture of the reign of Queen Victoria, 1837-1901, sometimes extended to encompass the reign of William IV, 1830-37. A period of stylistic eclecticism in which Gothic (qv), Classical (qv) and other styles all had their proponents, resulting in the building of varied, and often colourful, structures.

winter garden Conservatory-style structure, often built of cast iron and glass; popular in the domestic context on a small scale, and as large-scale entertainment buildings (particularly at resorts), from the mid to late nineteenth century.

zigzag Norman (qv) decorative motif of a line turning sharply and alternately to right and left.

Bibliography

The North Riding and its Architecture

Frank Atkinson, *The Industrial Archaeology of North-East England Vols I & II* (David & Charles 1974).

M F Barbey, *Civil Engineering Heritage — Northern England* (Thomas Telford 1981).

Lionel Butler and Chris Given-Wilson, *Medieval Monasteries of Great Britain* (Michael Joseph 1983).

Oliver Carter, *An Illustrated History of British Railway Hotels 1838-1983* (Silver Link 1990).

Martin Collins, *Classic Walks on the North York Moors* (Oxford Illustrated Press 1990).

J H Crosby, *Ignatius Bonomi of Durham, Architect* (City of Durham Trust 1987).

Rosemary J Curry and Sheila Kirk, *Philip Webb in the North* (Teesside Polytechnic Press 1984).

Barry Harrison and Barbara Hutton, *Vernacular Houses in North Yorkshire and Cleveland* (John Donald 1984).

Gwyn Headley and Wim Meulenkamp, *Follies* (Jonathan Cape 1990).

J Robin Lidster, *Yorkshire Coast Lines* (Hendon Publishing 1983).

Timothy J Mickleburgh, *The Guide to British Piers* (Piers Information Bureau 1988).

Nikolaus Pevsner, *Yorkshire — The North Riding* (Penguin 1966).

William Page (ed), *Victoria County History — North Riding* (vol I, Constable 1914; vol II, St Catherine Press 1923).

Ian Sampson, *Cleveland Way* (Aurum Press 1989).

John Smith and Charlotte Haslam, *The Landmark Handbook* 1993 (Landmark Trust 1992).

A Wainwright, *A Coast to Coast Walk* (Westmorland Gazette 1973).

John K Walton, *The English Seaside Resort: A Social History 1750-1914* (Leicester University Press 1983).

John Woodhams, *Funicular Railways* (Shire Publications 1989).

The Land of the Ironmasters

Colin Cunningham, *Victorian and Edwardian Town Halls* (Routledge and Kegan Paul 1981).

Elizabeth M Green, 'On Change, Grandeur and Designs: The Early History of the Middlesbrough Exchange' (*Cleveland History* 50, spring 1986).

B J D Harrison and D W Pattenden, *Middlesbrough's History in Maps* (Cleveland and Teesside Local History Society 1980).

J K Harrison and A Harrison, 'Saltburn-by-the-Sea: The Early Years of a Stockton and
    Darlington Railway Company Venture' (*Industrial Archaeology Review* 4, 1980).
M W Kirby, *Men of Business and Politics* (Allen and Unwin 1984).
J W Leonard, 'Saltburn: The Northern Brighton', in E M Sigsworth (ed), *Ports and Resorts in the
    Regions* (Hull College of Higher Education 1980).
William Lillie, *The History of Middlesbrough* (Middlesbrough Corporation 1968).
Sally Maltby, Sally MacDonald and Colin Cunningham, *Alfred Waterhouse 1830—1905* (RIBA
    1983).
Norman McCord, *North East England — An Economic and Social History* (Batsford 1979).
Middlesbrough's Commercial Centre (Middlesbrough Borough Council 1987).
Callum Murray, 'Being on the Edge' (*Architects' Journal*, 15th August 1990).
Stephen Robbins, 'Arboreta in Cleveland: A Survey' (*Cleveland History* 59, autumn 1990).
John Wilford Wardell, *A History of Yarm* (J W Wardell 1957).
Lawrence Weaver, 'Acklam Hall, Yorkshire' (*Country Life*, 7th March 1914).
Chris Scott Wilson, *The History of Saltburn* (Seaside Books 1983).

666 Feet to the Captain's Column

J C Atkinson, *Forty Years in a Moorland Parish* (M T D Rigg Publications 1987).
E W Sockett, 'Yorkshire's Early Warning System, 1916-1936' (*Yorkshire Archaeological Journal*
    61, 1989)
Noreen Vickers, 'The Destruction of Medieval and Georgian Churches in and around
    Eskdale during the 18th and 19th Centuries' (*Cleveland History* 51, autumn 1986).

Crescent and Cell, Resort and Religion

Bill Breakell, *Stone Causeways of the North York Moors* (Footsteps Books 1982).
Jonathan Glancey, 'New wars, new horizons' (*The Independent*, 18th November 1992).
Michael Hall, 'Mount Grace Priory, Yorkshire' (*Country Life*, 16th September 1993).
R H Hayes and J G Rutter, *Wade's Causeway* (Scarborough Archaeological and Historical
    Society 1964)
Richard Muir, *Shell Guide to Reading the Landscape* (Michael Joseph 1981).
The Rievaulx Terrace (National Trust 1978).
Royal Commission on the Historical Monuments of England, *Houses of the North York Moors*
    (HMSO 1987).

Last Train to the Queen of the North

Bass, Ratcliff and Gretton Limited Excursion to Scarborough 1914 (Bass Museum 1977).
Mark Bence-Jones, '"Cheer the Spirits, Brace the Nerves"' (*Country Life*, 18th April 1974).
Mark Bence-Jones, '"Lavish Hospitality and Fun"' (*Country Life*, 2nd May 1974).
Mark Girouard, *Robert Smythson and the Elizabethan Country House* (Yale University Press 1983).

J McDonnell (ed), *A History of Helmsley, Rievaulx and District* (Stonegate Press 1963).
Lynn F Pearson, *The People's Palaces* (Barracuda Books 1991).
Scarborough Heritage Trail (Scarborough Borough Council 1984).
Charles Saumarez Smith, *The Building of Castle Howard* (Faber and Faber 1990).

Meandering Through the Vale
Philip and Dorothy Brown, 'Spanish Flavour in Church Tiles' (*Glazed Expressions* 25, winter 1992).
Beningbrough Hall (National Trust 1986).

Gothick Gems and a Plundered Dale
Alec Clifton-Taylor, *Six English Towns* (British Broadcasting Corporation 1978).
Robert T Clough, *The Lead Smelting Mills of the Yorkshire Dales and Northern Pennines* (Clough 1980).
R Fieldhouse and B Jennings, *A History of Richmond and Swaledale* (Phillimore 1978).
Jane Hatcher, *Richmondshire Architecture* (C J Hatcher 1990).
Giles Worsley, 'Aske Hall, Yorkshire' (*Country Life*, 1st and 8th March 1990).

Druids in a Dale of Follies
Marcus Binney, 'Bolton Castle, Yorkshire' (*Country Life*, 21st May 1992).

Index

Main entries are in **bold**; illustrations in *italics*.